BOULDER CITY LIBRARY

3 1432 00113 8781

I0688225

YA
725
.97
BAR

Barter, James

Tower of Pisa

DISCARD

Boulder City Library
7   s Boulevard
Boulder City, NV 89005

THE
TOWER
OF PISA

BUILDING
HISTORY
SERIES

THE
TOWER
OF PISA

by James Barter

Boulder City Library
701 Adams Boulevard
Boulder City, NV 89005

DISCARD

MAY   2005

Lucent Books, Inc., San Diego, California

Library of Congress Cataloging-in-Publication Data

Barter, James, 1946–
    The Tower of Pisa / by James Barter.
      p.   cm. — (Building history series)
Includes bibliographical references and index.
    ISBN 1-56006-874-4
    1. Leaning Tower (Pisa, Italy)—Juvenile literature. 2. Bell
towers—Italy—Pisa—Juvenile literature. 3. Architecture,
Romanesque—Italy—Pisa—Juvenile literature. 4. Pisa (Italy)—
Buildings, structures, etc.—Juvenile literature. [1. Leaning Tower
(Pisa, Italy) 2. Pisa (Italy)—Buildings, structures, etc.] I. Title. II.
Series.
    NA5621.P716 B37 2001
    725'.97'094555—dc21

00-012611

Copyright 2001 by Lucent Books, Inc.
P.O. Box 289011, San Diego, California, 92198-9011

No part of this book may be reproduced or used in any other form
or by any other means, electrical, mechanical, or otherwise, including, but not limited to, photocopy, recording, or any information
storage and retrieval system, without prior written permission from
the publisher.

Printed in the U.S.A.

CONTENTS

FOREWORD

Throughout history, as civilizations have evolved and prospered, each has produced unique buildings and architectural styles. Combining the need for both utility and artistic expression, a society's buildings, particularly its large-scale public structures, often reflect the individual character traits that distinguish it from other societies. In a very real sense, then, buildings express a society's values and unique characteristics in tangible form. As scholar Anita Abramovitz comments in her book *People and Spaces*, "Our ways of living and thinking—our habits, needs, fear of enemies, aspirations, materialistic concerns, and religious beliefs—have influenced the kinds of spaces that we build and that later surround and include us."

That specific types and styles of structures constitute an outward expression of the spirit of an individual people or era can be seen in the diverse ways that various societies have built palaces, fortresses, tombs, churches, government buildings, sports arenas, public works, and other such monuments. The ancient Greeks, for instance, were a supremely rational people who originated Western philosophy and science, including the atomic theory and the realization that the earth is a sphere. Their public buildings, epitomized by Athens's magnificent Parthenon temple, were equally rational, emphasizing order, harmony, reason, and above all, restraint.

By contrast, the Romans, who conquered and absorbed the Greek lands, were a highly practical people preoccupied with acquiring and wielding power over others. The Romans greatly admired and readily copied elements of Greek architecture, but modified and adapted them to their own needs. "Roman genius was called into action by the enormous practical needs of a world empire," wrote historian Edith Hamilton. "Rome met them magnificently. Buildings tremendous, indomitable, amphitheaters where eighty thousand could watch a spectacle, baths where three thousand could bathe at the same time."

In medieval Europe, God heavily influenced and motivated the people, and religion permeated all aspects of society, molding people's worldviews and guiding their everyday actions. That spiritual mindset is reflected in the most important medieval structure—the Gothic cathedral—which, in a sense, was a model of heavenly cities. As scholar Anne Fremantle so elegantly phrases it, the cathedrals were "harmonious elevations of stone and glass reaching up to heaven to seek and receive the light [of God]."

Our more secular modern age, in contrast, is driven by the realities of a global economy, advanced technology, and mass communications. Responding to the needs of international trade and the growth of cities housing millions of people, today's builders construct engineering marvels, among them towering skyscrapers of steel and glass, mammoth marine canals, and huge and elaborate rapid transit systems, all of which would have left their ancestors, even the Romans, awestruck.

In examining some of humanity's greatest edifices, Lucent Books' Building History series recognizes this close relationship between a society's historical character and its buildings. Each volume in the series begins with a historical sketch of the people who erected the edifice, exploring their major achievements as well as the beliefs, customs, and societal needs that dictated the variety, functions, and styles of their buildings. A detailed explanation of how the selected structure was conceived, designed, and built, to the extent that this information is known, makes up the majority of the volume.

Each volume in the Lucent Building History series also includes several special features that are useful tools for additional research. A chronology of important dates gives students an overview, at a glance, of the evolution and use of the structure described. Sidebars create a broader context by adding further details on some of the architects, engineers, and construction tools, materials, and methods that made each structure a reality, as well as the social, political, and/or religious leaders and movements that inspired its creation. Useful maps help the reader locate the nations, cities, streets, and individual structures mentioned in the text; and numerous diagrams and pictures illustrate tools and devices that bring to life various stages of construction. Finally, each volume contains two bibliographies, one for student research, the other listing works the author consulted in compiling the book.

Taken as a whole, these volumes, covering diverse ancient and modern structures, constitute not only a valuable research tool, but also a tribute to the human spirit, a fascinating exploration of the dreams, skills, ingenuity, and dogged determination of the great peoples who shaped history.

Important Dates in the Building of the Tower of Pisa

1173–1178
Work progresses until 1178, when the tower is just over three stories tall; a two-inch tilt to the north is first identified.

1933
Engineers drill 361 holes into the masonry foundation and inject one hundred tons of concrete to seal the foundation from an underground spring; this mistake destabilizes the tower, causing a more dramatic tilt.

1360–1370
The last story, the belfry, is completed; the southward lean is almost four feet.

| 1100 | 1200 | 1300 | 1800 | 1900 | 1990 |

1272–1278
Work continues until 1278, when the seventh floor is completed; the tower tilts to the south roughly 2.5 feet.

1909
Precise measurements of the tower indicate a thirteen-foot lean.

1817
The tower's lean is measured at about twelve feet off the vertical line.

1990
The tower is closed to the public out of fears of its collapse; the seventeenth Pisa Commission is formed to find a solution.

8

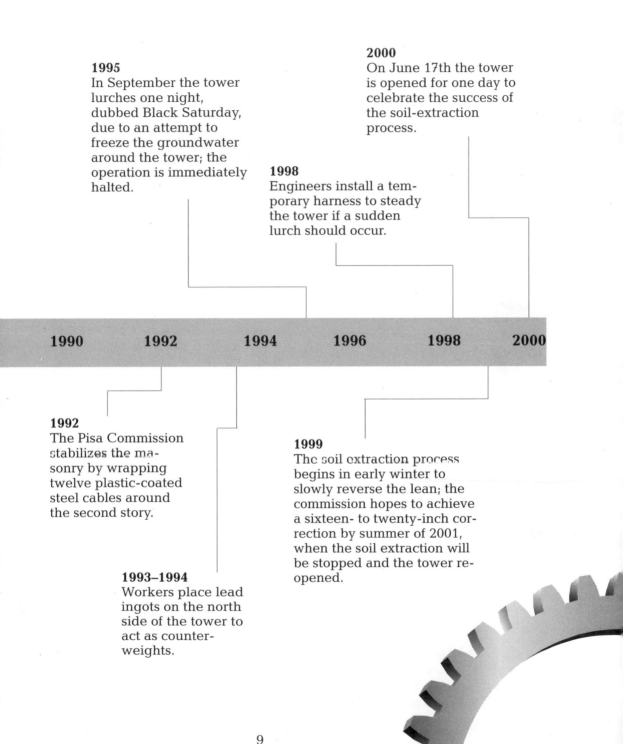

1995
In September the tower lurches one night, dubbed Black Saturday, due to an attempt to freeze the groundwater around the tower; the operation is immediately halted.

2000
On June 17th the tower is opened for one day to celebrate the success of the soil-extraction process.

1998
Engineers install a temporary harness to steady the tower if a sudden lurch should occur.

| 1990 | 1992 | 1994 | 1996 | 1998 | 2000 |

1992
The Pisa Commission stabilizes the masonry by wrapping twelve plastic-coated steel cables around the second story.

1999
The soil extraction process begins in early winter to slowly reverse the lean; the commission hopes to achieve a sixteen- to twenty-inch correction by summer of 2001, when the soil extraction will be stopped and the tower re-opened.

1993–1994
Workers place lead ingots on the north side of the tower to act as counter-weights.

INTRODUCTION

Many architects and engineers believe that the world-famous Leaning Tower of Pisa, voted one of the seven engineering wonders of the Middle Ages, also qualifies as one of the seven engineering blunders of the Middle Ages. Remarkably elegant as its 193-foot-tall silhouette penetrates the northern Italian sky, the tower nonetheless appears to be close to falling over because of a lean that began during its construction over eight hundred years ago.

The Leaning Tower is the leading attraction in Pisa, a small university town on Italy's Arno River. Built in the Piazza dei Miracoli—the Plaza of Miracles—the tower, along with Pisa's cathedral and baptistery, form a matched set of quintessential Pisan Romanesque architecture. Of the three, the tower attracts 90 percent of the seven hundred thousand tourists annually drawn to this city.

Located in the Piazza dei Miracoli, the Leaning Tower of Pisa, along with the city's baptistery and cathedral, are impressive examples of Pisan Romanesque architecture.

The tower's attraction lies neither with its elegant colonnades of Carrara marble, nor the eight symmetrical stories of alternating arches and gleaming columns, nor for the purpose for
which it was built: The chiming of its bells. Visitors who flock
here largely overlook the aesthetic qualities of the tower in favor
of gawking at what is arguably one of the world's most famous
building defects—a seventeen-foot lean.

The Tower of Pisa deserves better. It was conceived at a
time when Pisa's commercial success was soaring and the city's
leaders adorned their community with architectural jewels ex-
pressing its prestige to visitors and to residents alike. Because
the tower was built next to the existing cathedral and baptistery that showed no signs of leaning, its architect and builders
had no reason to assume that their latest masterpiece would be
different.

History is replete with such assumptions that have proved to
be fateful. The architect of the tower, generally accepted by art
historians to have been Bonanno Pisano, specified a foundation
depth of ten feet, which, by today's engineering standards,
would have been sufficient to carry the tower's weight if the soil
were compact. As the digging of the foundation proceeded,
workmen removed bucketfuls of moist, mucky clay and silt deposited by the nearby Arno River. This must have concerned
Pisano because excavations of the foundation reveal a sixteen-
inch layer of gravel commonly used to give support to soft soil.
However, Pisano apparently saw no reason to do more.

Construction work moved ahead at full speed in 1173, and
the first, second, and third stories glistened in the Pisan sun at a
height of seventy-two feet before a war temporarily halted the
project after five years. As the workers all went their separate
ways to await the end of the war, there was discussion about a
slight two-inch lean. No one was too concerned, however, since
the lean was merely two inches; other buildings in the piazza
were level, and besides, the problem might correct itself.

By the time work resumed on the bell tower in 1272, Pisano
was dead. And those two inches, much like an illness, did not
heal. The two inches became four, then eight, then several feet,
and then several yards. In 1990 a commission of internationally
acclaimed engineers began a ten-year project to first understand the nature of the tower's malady, and then to heal it. Eight
hundred years after Pisano began this lovely tower, the truth

Built on moist clay and silt deposited by the nearby Arno River, the Tower of Pisa has acquired a lean of seventeen feet.

about it and his oversight have come to light. Armed with modern technology, members of the commission probed, measured, and monitored the tower until they not only discovered the cause of the famous seventeen-foot lean, but also, more importantly, proposed a cure.

1

PISAN HISTORY AND TWELFTH-CENTURY ROMANESQUE ARCHITECTURE

Located in the verdant northwest region of Italy known for its many rivers and gentle sloping valleys, the city of Pisa sits ten miles inland from the Ligurian Sea, which lies just north of the Tyrrhenian Sea. Never large enough or successful enough to control its own destiny, Pisa was often subordinated to more powerful cities and civilizations.

Pisa began as an Etruscan town some time around the fourth century B.C. The Etruscans who dominated this region are of obscure origin because little of their writing exists and what does exist is difficult to translate. At some point around the second century B.C. Pisa became a Roman colony when the city of Rome conquered the Etruscans.

Rome had quickly grown in strength to the point where its well-disciplined armies swept over and viciously defeated all adversaries on the Italian peninsula, including Pisa. With Italy firmly under control, Rome looked south to Carthage, across the Mediterranean on the coast of North Africa. Master of much of the western Mediterranean, Carthage was a powerful trading colony of the Phoenicians, a civilization on the eastern coast of the Mediterranean in what is today Lebanon. Following three major wars between 264 and 146 B.C., Rome crushed Carthage and, not yet satisfied, turned its gaze to venerable Greece and the eastern Mediterranean. By the second century A.D., every

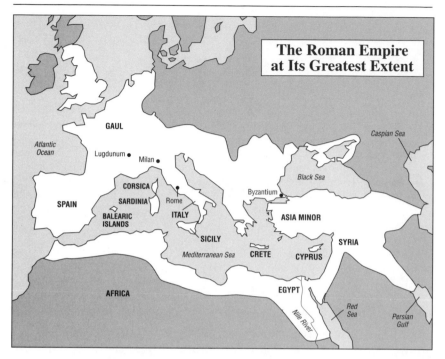

inch of land touched by the warm Mediterranean waters lay within Rome's grasp, as did the cold, mountainous lands to the north.

Rome's fortunes rose and fell over time and finally, at the end of the fifth century A.D., its leaders could no longer successfully maintain their grip over the expansive empire. Germanic tribes began spilling across its borders rushing headlong through Pisa and other northern Italian cities on their way to sack and destroy a wounded and abandoned Rome. Historians recognize the date of A.D. 476 as the end of the Roman Empire. The emperor that year, Romulus Augustulus, was the last.

The eventual collapse of the Roman Empire ushered in the historical period known as the Middle Ages. As the collapse gradually took place, the prosperity and security that European cities and villages had enjoyed for hundreds of years under the protective umbrella of the Roman Empire vanished. Nothing replaced Rome's army, laws, currency, or universal Latin language, leaving much of Europe without a social or political structure to ensure continued prosperity and achievement. The unity and quality of life that Europe had enjoyed under the Roman Empire lay shattered just as a sheet of glass dropped to the floor splits into hundreds of disconnected fragments.

Unbeknownst to Pisans and the rest of Europe at this time, another major force was in its infancy that, within three hundred years, would place its stamp on European history in the form of large-scale warfare that would continue for centuries. This force, the founding of a new religion following the teachings of the prophet Muhammad, was quietly gaining support in the Middle East and along the North African coast of the Mediterranean. The followers of this new religion, called Muslims, were as yet a small minority, but in time they would challenge European Christians for control of the entire Mediterranean basin as well as all of Europe. But this conflict was still many generations away, and Pisans had other matters to occupy their thoughts and aspirations.

Muhammad and his followers, called Muslims, fought Christians for control of Europe.

THE MIDDLE AGES

Without the protection and commercial support of the Roman Empire, Pisa and hundreds of other towns experienced a decline in their quality of life. Poverty and uncertainty plagued people's lives as most struggled to earn a meager living plowing fields behind oxen or running small shops in which they sold hand-crafted items of necessity. For the next three hundred years most of Europe remained essentially a primitive culture, furthering none of the innovations in literature, architecture, law, trade, or education that had been hallmarks of not only Roman civilization but Greek civilization as well.

This cultural decline, combined with the fragmentation of European communities, left the region militarily and economically weak and vulnerable to attack. During the late eighth and early ninth centuries, Muslims recognized this vulnerability and began a series of incursions across the Mediterranean into Spain, Italy, and France. A number of bloody battles were fought, finally driving the Muslims back to North Africa. One of these vicious wars pitted the allied armies of Pisa and Genoa against the Muslims, who had invaded two islands off the coast of Tuscany. After more than a hundred years of intermittent battles, the alliance drove the Muslims from the islands.

Some semblance of normalcy returned to northern Italy, but it would not last long. Initially Pisa and other coastal cities of northern Italy prospered from trade with cities in the western and eastern Mediterranean. But the Muslim armies reasserted themselves in the middle of the tenth century, when they conquered an area in the eastern Mediterranean known to Europeans as the Holy Land. Christians revered this land as the place Jesus lived, taught, and died. They made frequent pilgrimages there to pay homage to his teachings. The Muslim conquest ended these pilgrimages, cutting off Christians from their most sacred landmarks. When the Roman Catholic pope received news of this affront, he proclaimed a holy war that would have far-reaching effects on Pisa and nearly all of its neighboring cities.

THE CRUSADES

This holy war, known as the Crusades, was a series of military expeditions intended to recapture the Holy Land from the Muslims. Between 1095 and 1270, kings and princes throughout Europe pledged tens of thousands of warriors to aid in this quest. Initially the Crusaders experienced success against the Muslims, but eventually they were defeated.

Even though Christian soldiers lost the military wars against the Muslims, Christian traders in Pisa and Venice prospered as a

Crusaders (left) battled Muslims for control of the Holy Land between 1095 and 1270.

Minted in Florence, the florin became the standard currency for all of Europe for hundreds of years.

result of the Crusades. Crusading armies returned home to sell at great profit the goods they had acquired in the Middle East. Pisan ships carrying soldiers to the war returned home loaded with exotic commodities that propelled their owners into the ranks of millionaires. Beautiful clothing made of colorful silk; spices that dazzled taste buds; wines, fruits, and vegetables never before imagined; and finely carved wood furniture filled the marketplaces of northern Italy.

As trade flourished in Pisa, shipbuilders, ship owners, and traders began amassing unprecedented fortunes. They used these increasingly large personal fortunes to pioneer the lending of money at high interest rates, allowing them to profit not only at their professions but also on their surplus money. Similarly, in Florence, the banking and lending industries became so profitable that the city minted its own gold coin, called the florin, which became the standard currency for all of Europe for hundreds of years. Powerful banking and shipping families in Pisa, Florence, and Venice became famous for their massive fortunes.

One of the secondary benefits of this commercial success was a phenomenal outpouring of money from wealthy merchants to build larger and more ornate civic buildings meant both to beautify and bring respect to their cities. Pisa, like so many other northern Italian cities, began constructing ostentatious public buildings on a grand scale to dazzle the locals and impress visitors from rival towns, who would return home with stories of awe-inspiring architecture.

ROMANESQUE ARCHITECTURE

When Pisan architects began their grand period of building in the mid–eleventh century, the architectural style of the time was called Romanesque. Although this ornate style was derived from the architecture of ancient Rome (hence its name), it had evolved from a much simpler style following the collapse of the Roman Empire in the late fifth century.

The political and social turbulence that followed the collapse of the Roman Empire forced architects to construct small

A Romanesque vault forms a ceiling over an interior area of the San Martin de Fromista, an eleventh-century Spanish church.

buildings with thick, unadorned, windowless walls. Such walls offered protection for the next five hundred years, when invasions, sieges of cities, and subsequent looting and burning were common. Flammable wooden roofs were abandoned in favor of vaults similar to those once constructed by the Romans.

The vault is one of the most significant Romanesque architectural elements. It forms a ceiling over a large interior area while supporting the weight of the roof. A vault is shaped like a large arch and is usually made of stone and concrete. Marble

The restored peace of the tenth century freed architects to decorate structures with windows such as this one at the Saint-Pierre Parish Church of Mont-Saint-Michel in France.

columns may support small vaults, but large vaults require the greater strength of stone piers and walls. Vaults are most commonly found in large structures built to accommodate large numbers of people, such as cathedrals, courthouses, and other public meetinghouses.

The earliest evidence of the use of this vaulting style during the Middle Ages indicates that it was initially confined to small rooms. Architects who experimented with larger vaults soon replaced the delicate support columns with stronger stone piers necessary to support the increasingly heavy stone and concrete ceiling. Medieval architects relearned what the Romans had known many centuries earlier, that the vault and the pier are the keys to supporting vast open interior spaces needed for large gatherings of people.

Around the tenth century, the period of wars finally ended and people no longer feared invading armies. This turn of events restored peace and security to northern Italy and ended the need for small, thick-walled, windowless structures. Architects could now confidently design larger cathedrals with windows that flooded the interiors with light.

As architects integrated more and more windows into cathedral designs, the walls became weaker. To prevent them from collapsing, architects designed increasingly sophisticated vaults capable of transferring the weight of the ceiling away from the windows and the walls. Large cathedrals, baptisteries, and other public structures with many windows and ornate vaults began gracing the landscape.

When large interior open spaces were not needed, however, smaller interior spaces such as those found in bell towers, were supported by arches and columns. These two elements were capable of supporting small roofs and colonnades and had the design advantage of appearing to be light and elegant—just what Pisan designers needed for the decorative elements of their Romanesque tower.

ARCHES

The arch is an architectural element, usually made of stone and concrete, that is built on two legs that gradually curve toward a center meeting point. The arch's function is to support the

CARRARA MARBLE

Of all of the different types and colors of marble quarried in Italy, none is more widely used by builders and sculptors than that found in Carrara, a city in north central Italy. Here, an entire mountain of famous white marble has been quarried by generations of local quarrymen, who have provided marble for virtually all major monuments in Italy as well as for many of the most famous sculptors of the Renaissance, such as Michelangelo, Donatello, and Bernini.

Steep mountains surround Carrara on all sides, and the cuts into these mountains of marble give the landscape a smooth, white, glacial appearance. The quarrying of marble begins with the drilling of dozens of deep holes along a straight line close to the edge of a shelf. Small charges of dynamite are set in the holes, and at a signal all are detonated, releasing a massive sheet of Carrara marble down the side of the mountain. Although the enormous sheet breaks into pieces, they weigh many tons and are trucked to one of the many fabrication plants. At such plants, the large blocks are run through a bank of ten to fifteen diamond-studded circular saw blades, each evenly spaced, that slice through the marble like a bread cutter.

After the finished slabs are polished, they are shipped all around the world for builders and carvers to complete. Many sculptors still believe that Carrara marble, known as "the Marble of Michelangelo" because the artist used it for his statue of David and many of his other famous works, is the best marble for sculptures.

VAULTS

Vaults defined the Romanesque style of architecture more than any other feature. Vaults were designed to support a roof over a large, open area. Romanesque engineers designed three different types of vaults, each an improvement over its predecessor. They were named the barrel vault, the groin vault, and the cross-ribbed vault.

The barrel vault is so named because, when viewing it from the floor, it has the shape of a large barrel that has been cut in half down the length and then used as a ceiling. The barrel vault was significant because it allowed for a long, fireproof, concrete-and-stone roof to cover a very large room. As barrel vaults grew in size and increased in weight, thicker walls were constructed to bear the heavy load of the tons of stone and concrete.

Stone arch rings, called groin vaults, were added to lend additional support for the large barrel vaults. Their purpose was to transfer the downward pressure away from the walls, bringing it down these arch rings, which in turn transferred it to the floor. They were added to the interior of the barrel vault, running up one side of the vault, across the top, and down the other side. Set roughly every twenty to thirty feet along the inside length of the barrel, small columns or piers were added on each side to support the arch rings.

As groin vaults came into use, heavy, solid walls gave way to walls with windows that illuminated the interiors of

weight above an opening such as a doorway. The Romans deserve most of the credit for the development of the arch, even though primitive ones date to much earlier times. The more the Romans experimented with arches, the stronger yet lighter they became. When the Pisans began their building program, they had many styles of Roman arches to copy.

Pisan architects designed arches for their buildings because of their gracefulness as well as their structural strength. Initially strength was more important than gracefulness, but by the time architects began building in the eleventh century, the opposite was true. The most common types of arches built during this great building period were open arches, used to support the

the cathedrals during the day. Worshipers could for the first time enjoy the interior beauty of these great cathedrals.

However, the addition of windows weakened the walls, causing them to collapse under the weight of the roofs. Rather than reduce the numbers of windows, medieval engineers added cross ribs for greater support. The last of the great Romanesque innovations, cross-ribbed vaulting relieved more of the weight of the ceiling, carrying the weight down the ribs and away from the walls.

As the use of the ribbed vault evolved, delicate double and triple ribs replaced the one heavy rib and decorative rosettes broke up the monotony of the long, arching ribs. Beauty and function were both served as large Romanesque buildings added more and more windows to bathe their interiors in light.

Ribbed vaults adorn the outside of the Abbey of Fontenay in Burgundy, France.

colonnades found on each building in the Piazza dei Miracoli, and closed arches that were merely decorative.

Open arches are freestanding and allow people to see through them. They are found on colonnades, which are covered walkways designed to protect people from the sun and rain. To build the colonnades, designers placed the roof on open arches supported by columns. These arches were round at the top and were usually spaced about six to eight feet apart. They were prized in Pisa because they were often beautifully carved from white Carrara marble and looked artistic while supporting the roof.

Sometimes architects wanted only the appearance of an arch for decorative purposes. When this occurred, architects

Supported by open arches, colonnades span the façade of the cathedral in the Piazza dei Miracoli.

built what was called a blind arch. Blind arches were carved three to six inches deep into large walls without going all the way through. Architects used them to decorate what would otherwise be large, monotonous walls. Unlike the open arch, the blind arch had no function. Although blind arches were also abundantly found on Pisan architecture, they were not freestanding, they did not support a roof, and they could not be looked through.

Arches were one of the most important elements for Pisan architects, just as were columns. Open arches were usually supported by columns, and as the design of arches changed over time, so did the design of columns.

COLUMNS

The columns that Pisan architects designed to support the weight of their roofs and arches have a long history that goes back to the ancient Egyptians. However, it was the Greeks who elevated columns to an art form by developing three distinctive styles, called orders.

The three orders are distinguished by the design of the three major elements of a column: the capital, the column shaft, and the base. The capital is the topmost element that sits between the column shaft and the roof or vault that it supports. The column shaft

The baptistery in Pisa is carved with decorative blind arches.

Left: Doric columns support the roof of the Parthenon in Athens. Above: The fluted shaft and decorative scroll of an Ionic column. Below: Pilasters form an arch on the exterior of the Gelati Monastery in Russia.

transfers the weight of the roof from the capital to the base, and the base in turn transfers the weight to the ground.

The oldest order the Greeks designed is called Doric. It is recognized by the simplicity of its design, which many art historians believe makes it the most elegant and most beautiful order. The Doric capital is a square piece of marble without decoration. The column shaft may be plain or fluted and, unlike the other two orders, it does not have a base.

The second-oldest order is the Ionic. The square capital is easily identified by the decorative scroll design found at either two or all four of its sides. The column shaft is fluted, meaning decorative lines are carved in the shaft from the capital down to the base. The base is usually fairly simple, with a slight widening from the top of the base to the bottom.

The last order designed is the Corinthian. The Corinthian capital is the most recognizable of the three orders because of its ornate design that resembles long, thin acanthus leaves that curl at the ends. The column shaft is fluted and the base dramatically widens from top to bottom.

The function of all of the columns, regardless of order, was to support weight, but sometimes Pisan architects wanted the look of a column without needing its strength. To solve this problem, they cut columns in half from top to bottom. These half columns are technically called pilasters. Architects then cemented the flat side of the pilaster directly against a wall creating the appearance of a column. Designers frequently set pilasters underneath blind arches to create an illusion of open arches supported by freestanding columns.

The rise of these new styles during the later part of the tenth and early eleventh centuries led to a great outburst of building in Pisa, other Italian towns, and throughout Europe. These designs were a welcome break from the designs of earlier periods, which gave many structures the appearance of fortresses. The new light look of marble was welcomed after centuries of heavy stone and brick. In tenth-century Pisa, the citizens who took pride in their cathedral and baptistery were anxious to begin the bell tower.

TOWERS

The function of all medieval towers like the Tower of Pisa, as well as those preceding the Middle Ages, was deeply rooted in communications and war. The function of the earliest known towers, dating back thirty-five hundred years to Greece, was to transmit critical information, usually of a military nature, over long distances as quickly as possible. To accomplish this, the Greeks signaled with fire to announce the result of a battle.

Before any important faraway battle, military leaders explained to everyone at home that if the battle were successful, a fire signal would be sent announcing the victory. A chain of fire towers, spaced about ten miles apart, accomplished the transmission of the victory signal. Standing tall on flat plains or perched high on mountaintops where they could be seen for many miles, each tower stored a bundle of wood on a platform. If and when the victory occurred, the first tower in the chain lit its fire, announcing the victory to the next tower. This sequence repeated itself until the victory signal reached its final destination. Defeated armies walked home without sending a message.

The ancient Greek writer Aeschylus tells the story of King Agamemnon's return home to Greece after the ten-year war against the Trojans. His homecoming was communicated to his wife, Clytemnestra, who awaited his return. As Aeschylus tells the story in his play *Agamemnon*, fire towers rimmed the Aegean Sea and a watchman at each tower awaited the signal that would announce the destruction of Troy and the return of their king:

> I wait; to read the meaning in that beacon light, a blaze
> of fire to carry out of Troy the rumor . . . of its capture. Oh

hail, blaze of the darkness. . . . I cry the news to Agamemnon's queen [Clytemnestra] that she may rise up . . . to the rumor of gladness welcoming this beacon, and singing rise, if truly the citadel of Ilium [Troy] has fallen, as the shining of this fire proclaims.[1]

Two thousand years after the Trojan War, the Romans had not advanced communications much and still used fire towers to telegraph information along the length of the Italian coast to Rome. The average time to start a signal fire after receiving a signal was about thirty minutes. The average distance of ten miles between towers meant a signal could be broadcast over a two-hundred-mile distance in about ten hours; roughly the equivalent of one entire night. This assumes everything worked according to plan, which it rarely did. Watchmen falling asleep and rainy nights were only two of the problems with fire towers.

CHURCH BELL TOWERS

The collapse of the Roman Empire at the end of the fifth century A.D. brought an end to the use of fire towers for communications. People no longer needed to communicate across thousands of miles throughout the Roman Empire but only across a mile or two within small medieval towns. As Rome declined in authority, Christian

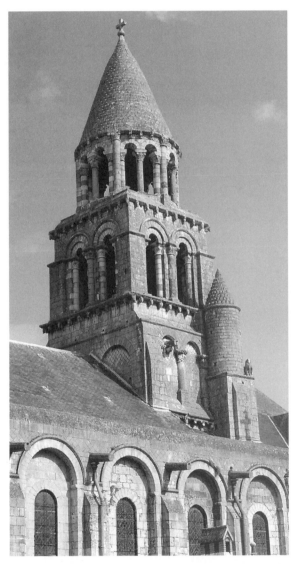

Church bell towers such as this one built on the Church of Notre Dame la Grande in Poitiers, France, replaced fire towers as the major means of communication.

MEDIEVAL CLOCKS

During the Middle Ages the time of day was announced to communities by bells, but the bells did not keep the time. Bell ringers did not strike the time of day until a timepiece of some sort indicated it was time to do so. Time was kept by many methods, some as imprecise as observing the position of the sun as it moved across the sky, and others far more precise using human constructed devices.

Farmers generally scheduled their daily activities around the position of the sun in the sky. Accuracy to within an hour was generally sufficient, but when the sun went down, they had no way of knowing the time except to guess. In a simple rural existence, farmers were satisfied with this imprecise method because they rarely attended meetings or other occasions requiring punctuality. Such a situation was not the case in cities.

Life in medieval cities had much of the urgency and many of the complexities of modern city life. Coordinating family activities as well as business meetings required accurate time-keeping. The age of mechanical clocks was still several hundred years away, yet medieval families had several devices for telling time.

A statue of an angel with a sundial at Chartres Cathedral in France.

churches became increasingly important in the lives of the people as their most stable institution. As such, the church needed to communicate with all members of a village.

In such a setting, the use of bells as a means of communication made sense. Small church bells could be carried throughout a city and could be struck to tap out a primitive form of Morse code that conveyed messages to the citizens. As time passed and communities grew in size and population, it became necessary to communicate over greater distances. To achieve this, larger bells were made and housed in tall bell towers. From these structures, the bell ringers could communicate church messages over the roofs of smaller buildings and out into the community.

One of the more common devices for keeping fairly accurate time during daylight hours was the sundial. Still in use today in many agrarian communities, the sundial is usually a flat circular metal plate with the hours marked around the perimeter just like a modern analog clock. Protruding vertically from the center of the plate is a short rod, called a gnomon, that casts a shadow across the plate to indicate the time of day. As the sun moves across the sky, the shadow moves on the plate, reporting the changing time. The only drawback to the sundial was its dependence on the sun.

A second popular option that could be used night or day was the hourglass, which is made of glass shaped like the number eight. The top segment is filled with sand that drains into the bottom segment at a consistent rate. When the upper segment emptied, the hourglass was tipped over and the cycle started anew. An hourglass measured one hour or more, depending on its size. Large ones could measure a twenty-four-hour day before needing to be flipped over to measure the next twenty-four hours.

Other timekeeping options available to medieval families included candles that burned at prescribed rates and water clocks that allowed water to pass through a narrow pipe at a predetermined rate. All things considered, medieval life could be well measured.

BELLS AS MESSENGERS

As cities grew and prospered, city life became more complex and people needed still more messages to be kept informed of events in their villages. The single church bell was no longer sufficient to meet the needs of the community. To announce news more effectively, the single bell in the bell tower grew in number to several bells and finally to sometimes as many as twenty. Additional bells were always of different tones, and over time a summoning of the community with many bells indicated an event of greater importance than a summoning with a single bell.

This increase in the number of bells sometimes meant that the tone of a particular bell indicated the occasion for which it was being rung. For example, the specific bell that was sounded when someone died was called the death knell or the death bell. Percival Price, in his book *Bells and Man*, has this to say of the death bell:

> [The death bell] might break into anyone's activities, day or night, and when people heard it they stopped their work to pray for the soul of the one whose passing it signaled. Rung for the last earthly hours of a dying person, it is one of the most universal uses of the church bell.[2]

Bells were also used to summon people to mark the many passages in people's lives, both happy and sad. These announcements would be rung from small, local bell towers rather than from the large, citywide bells and were intended to call family and close friends to honor the person and occasions. The following two inscriptions, found carved on bells, provide insights into their many uses: "I to the church the living call and to the grave do summon all" and "Sometimes joy and sometimes sorrow, marriage today and death tomorrow."[3]

Bells were rung not only to make special announcements but also to convey the time of day. Hourly bell ringing kept medieval life organized and people's work habits synchronized with the rest of the community. Eleventh-century Pisa was a bustling seaport. Merchants, ships' captains, and work crews needed to coordinate their time for such tasks as meetings, loading and unloading ships, and carting perishable foods to market before they spoiled. All groups in the workforce depended upon the accurate ringing of the bells to meet their schedules.

CIVIC BELL TOWERS

Although the church was initially reluctant to allow the bells to be rung for any nonreligious purpose, communications became too important to cities to limit their bells' use to church ceremonies. Towns needed to defend themselves from aggressive neighboring towns as well as from roving bands of marauders that would rob them of anything they could carry off. As historian Price reports,

> In the year 610, when the army of the Frankish [French] King, Clothaire II, approached Sens, [a city] near Paris, its bishop, St. Loup, rang his cathedral bell to summon

Civic bell towers such as the one at Palazzo Vecchio in Florence, Italy, were used to make public announcements.

the citizens to defend the city. This is but the first of many records of church authorities ringing their bells to rouse the people to their defense against soldiers or marauders.[4]

By the eleventh century many cities either used the bell towers of churches for civic announcements or had built separate bell towers for such uses. The addition of a second set of bells to a city did not confuse the citizens because the civic bells were cast to emit different tones from the religious ones. People could easily distinguish the differences between them.

THE ALARM BELL

The daily ringing of church bells, blending with the sounds of the civic bells, made for a mix that all citizens, even children, quickly memorized. The bells created village music that conveyed the general status of the city. The sounds of bells tolling throughout the city normally signified that all was well. But sometimes there was the sound of a bell so different that it caused every man, woman, and child to cease immediately whatever each was doing. Different in quality and in frequency, the tone of this low, dark bell was unmistakable, and when it was struck, all other bells immediately ceased their peals. It was the alarm bell.

The deep booming sound of the alarm bell resonated farther than any other bell. Its tone was intended to frighten the villagers because it signaled approaching danger, either from an enemy or a natural disaster. When it sounded, every citizen went to his or her post either to defend the city or to prepare to help the injured and dying. Severe penalties were prescribed for those who disobeyed the alarm bell; in times of war the penalty was death.

Following the defeat of the enemy or the passing of the natural disaster, the bell signal for victory tolled. Unlike the alarm signal, this was not one single unique bell but rather a cacophony of all bells ringing together in a tumultuous symphony of sound. This was the only instance when all bells were rung continuously.

In time bell towers took on yet another function besides communications: that of defense. This came about because, in the absence of the law and order that the now-collapsed Roman Empire had provided, nomadic tribes migrated across the European landscape plundering cities, and aggressive towns raided their neighbors. Commercially prosperous medieval towns of northern Italy, such as Pisa, Venice, Lucca, San Gimignano, and Florence, had the most to lose and needed a way to combat this threat.

Towns first tried bargaining with the aggressors by offering them money and goods to go away. This, however, merely encouraged them to return. Hiding was no better, and fighting them was often worse. After one or two experiences with loss of life and property, cities came up with the idea, by no means new, of building walls around their cities for defense. Bell towers would soon become a critical part of this defense strategy.

BELL CASTING

The casting of bells during the Middle Ages was an old art form generally performed by the same local craftsman who made pots and pans. Most medieval bells were cast from bronze, a combination of copper and tin.

To create a good bell, the pot maker employed what is called the lost-wax process, which is thousands of years old. The craftsman first carved a clay model of the bell and then tightly wrapped it with a layer of wax several inches thick. He then covered the layer of wax with a heavy coating of plaster. When the three layers of clay, wax, and plaster were completed, the maker built a wood fire around the composition. As the fire heated the work, the wax melted and ran out a hole in the bottom, leaving a space between the clay and plaster. The bell maker then filled this space with bronze that had been heated to a liquid state. After the bronze cooled, the plaster and clay were removed to reveal the finished bronze bell.

A good bell maker could design a bell to a particular pitch by controlling the composition of the bronze and the bell shape. Generally, the composition of the bronze was roughly a ratio of thirteen parts of copper to four of tin. Increasing the ratio of tin could improve the tone but weakened the bell, increasing the possibility of cracking when the bell was first rung. If the ring of the finished bell was in need of adjustment, the bell maker chipped away small amounts of bronze from the interior of the bell until the desired tone was achieved.

The bell maker carved his name in the bell, and the local priest then consecrated it before it was hung in its permanent place. The consecration was a process similar to a baptism, with holy water followed by an incantation that called for the bell to ward off all acts of the devil as well as the destructive effects of hail, lightning, and wind. These last two acts lend a great deal of insight into the importance of the bells in the medieval city.

DEFENSE BELL TOWERS

Initially the combination of stone walls and the defensive use of the bell towers turned away most attackers. The ideal place for the defense towers was at the city gates, as author Percival Price explains:

> The early Norman tower of St. Michael's . . . was both the bell tower of a church and a watch tower at the north gate, and when the city was attacked its bell summoned both archers to pour arrows down on the enemy from the top and non-combatants to say prayers inside the church. . . . In war time every church tower became potentially a defense tower, and in villages, usually the only one. . . . Its top platform offered the best lookout for spotting the enemy, and its thick-walled lower portion the safest place for storing valuables against damage and plunder.[5]

This fresco by Benozzo Gozzoli (1420–1497) illustrates how defense bell towers were incorporated into city walls to help turn away invaders.

The defense bell tower located at the end of this medieval wall in Nordingen, Germany, was built to protect the city from violent attacks.

In time, however, invaders became increasingly persistent and sophisticated with siege machines. These machines were invented to knock holes in walls using a variety of techniques, such as battering rams and catapults capable of hurling huge stones. Violent attacks that destroyed walls gradually forced towns to construct stronger fortifications. Bell towers began to be incorporated into the fortification walls of cities to greatly enhance their ability to ward off invaders. Spaced along perimeter walls, these towers protruded out several feet from the wall and extended up many feet above them. This design allowed defenders to use their bows and arrows against attackers at the walls, provided them with a second line of defense in the event that attackers succeeded in breaching the walls, and signaled to other towers and to the citizenry in the midst of the fray.

Over the years Pisa and many other walled cities in the province of Tuscany and elsewhere in northern Italy continued to prosper and grow. Commerce continued to flourish, and as wealthy merchants and church officials sought to build ever more elaborate homes, larger shops, and more ornate churches, cities spilled beyond their walls. City walls therefore became ineffective for protection and the idea of expanding them was not

SIEGE MACHINES

Roving bands of marauders began attacking unprotected medieval cities during the early periods of the Middle Ages. As the attacks increased in numbers and ferocity, the townspeople built stone walls around their cities to protect themselves from attackers. Initially the walls were not very tall and invaders built ladders to scale them. Sometimes, attackers even tunneled under narrow walls to surprise the citizens inside. But as the walls grew higher and thicker, the attackers were forced to abandon ladders and tunnels in favor of more elaborate equipment.

Invaders designed siege machines to match the increasing height and thickness of city walls. These machines were designed to break through the walls either at close range or from a distance. If invaders could attack a wall at close quarters, the battering ram was the best offensive weapon. But if defenders using bow and arrows and other assortments of weapons were able to keep the invaders away from the wall, catapults were used.

Battering rams were simpler and more primitive than catapults. The battering ram is one of the oldest siege machines, dating back to the ancient Egyptians. It is built from a sturdy tree trunk, with one end protected by a hard metal cap. The principle behind the battering ram was to slam the capped only costly but also futile since the walls would have to be re-built repeatedly as the town grew.

So, cities abandoned the protection of the walls. Instead, they scattered defensive towers throughout the city. It was not un-usual for cities to have a dozen or more to protect everyone. Oc-casionally large families built towers exclusively for their own use.

As families began building their own defense towers, they decorated them to distinguish them from the towers of rival fam-ilies. Eventually the bell tower took one last evolutionary step. Prominent citizens now began viewing their towers not only as means of communication and defense but also as great state-ments, visible from many miles away, announcing the wealth and superiority of their city.

---

end of the ram against the wall repeatedly until a breach was created. Groups of men were able to pound walls using small rams, but the larger, more effective rams were attached to overhead beams with ropes that men could swing back and forth. The biggest drawback of the battering ram was that the men operating it were vulnerable to attack from the defend-ers above.

Attacking walls at a distance was safer for the attackers, but it required more elaborate siege machines. Catapult de-signs varied, but they all had the same purpose—to hurl a heavy object as far and as accurately as possible. Large cat-apults were built on carriages with wheels and were pulled by horses. One design copied the principle of the archery bow. A flexible iron bar was bent back, placing great tension on it, and when it reached its maximum tension, it was re-leased, hurling either a stone or javelin several hundred feet.

The second type of catapult looked like a huge wooden spoon. The handle end was firmly fixed in place on a plat-form with a large piece of timber in the middle. The broad end of the spoon was then winched down, creating tremen-dous pressure on the broad end. When the winch was sud-denly released, a stone in the broad end of the spoon was catapulted through the air.

PRESTIGE

As the commercial fortunes of northern Italian cities such as Pisa rose and the population expanded, prosperous members of the communities lavishly doled out the funds to build impressive buildings. To the local citizens these elegant buildings advertised the wealth and prestige of these families, and to outside visitors the architecture expressed civic pride.

As independent cities began to spread across the northern Italian countryside, they competed to build the tallest and most grandiose structures. They wanted to have the largest and most elaborate bell towers, and in many cases they also wanted to build more of them than any other city. Just as a modern city might enjoy the prestige of having the tallest building in the world, during the Middle Ages cities wanted the prestige of having the largest and most beautiful bell tower. The leaders of Florence hired the famous Renaissance painter and architect

Left: This Florence, Italy, bell tower was built by Renaissance painter and architect Giotto. Below: Thirteen bell towers dominate the skyline of San Gimignano, Italy.

Giotto to build a bell tower for their city because they wanted it to be more elaborate, taller, and more beautiful than the one built in the rival city of Pisa. The hill town of San Gimignano, south of Pisa, could boast of having seventy towers in its heyday, of which thirteen still pierce its rustic skyline.

TOWER DESIGNS

The earliest towers that were designed solely for bells were simple in design and as a rule were built beside the city's cathedral. During the early period of the Middle Ages, they were constructed of solid stone quarried from nearby hills and held together with cement without any decorative carvings or marble facing.

Early towers had either a square or rectangular base, although a few cylindrical ones can be found. All had a single wood door entry and a few narrow slits or open arches in the walls to admit interior light on the wood stairwell leading to the belfry. Up on top, the tower generally had a steeply pitched roof to keep water away from the supporting wood timbers, along with many arched openings in the perimeter walls to allow the unobstructed chiming of the bells to carry throughout the city.

On the belfry, the lone bell or occasionally multiple bells were attached to heavy timbers by iron spikes. Carpenters rounded the ends of the heavy timbers and set them in the open arches in the tower stone. Ringers pulled on ropes that rolled the bells over, causing their clappers to bang against the inside of the bell.

As bell towers evolved into defense towers, they took on the added responsibility of providing a place where warriors could keep the enemy at bay. The early examples of defensive bell towers differed from the regular bell towers in several significant structural ways. Built taller and with thicker walls than earlier bell towers, these defensive bell towers could withstand violent attacks. To minimize forced entry, the thick stone-block walls had only one main entry and no windows.

The doors, usually made of very heavy oak, were studded with iron spikes driven into them to prevent enemy axes and saws from cutting through the wood. The pitched roofs that were commonly found on earlier bell towers were removed to guard against them being set on fire and to create an extensive platform from which soldiers could attack invaders down below.

Early bell towers usually had rectangular bases, single wood door entries, narrow slits to provide interior light, and steeply pitched roofs.

Without windows, arches, pitched roofs, or any stone embellishments, these towers had the rugged look of sentries prepared to do battle.

Massive and simple, these towers were built to absorb brutal punishment without faltering. Catapults could hurl one-hundred-pound boulders against their walls without breaching them. Attempts to force defenders out by building bonfires around the towers also failed because of their stone construction. Sieges often lasted for months. For this reason, most defense towers were built over water wells and contained storage rooms for dry food and sleeping quarters on the upper levels.

In these towers, defenders could see the other towers and could signal back and forth. During a siege defenders rallied along the top of the tower, where notches cut into the wall, called crenellations, protected archers from enemy arrows. If there were window openings, they were high off the ground far from the reach of ladders. Defense took place from the top, where warriors could shoot arrows, drop heavy stones, throw down burning twigs, or pour boiling oil and water on unsuspecting attackers.

During sieges, city defenders could shoot arrows at attackers and drop stones, boiling water, and other objects on them from the tops of defense towers.

The design of the tower went through one final evolution as bell towers became status symbols advertising a city's wealth and cultural prestige. Unlike the thick, rustic, windowless defense towers, these beautifully articulated bell towers looked like wedding cakes or Christmas ornaments. To create these status symbols, cities bejeweled their bell towers in multicolored marble, graced them with delicate colonnades of marble columns, inset sculptured scenes depicting famous townspeople or historically significant events, and placed the towers prominently in the city's central piazza. In addition, these towers had not one major bell but many. Master bell makers were paid handsomely to cast bells with specific tones that communicated to the city in a melodious manner.

A structure in which a set of heavy bells were rung had to be capable of withstanding the lateral swing thrusts of tons of weight, necessitating stronger and larger towers. As medieval engineers designed towers with greater structural integrity,

Ornate bell towers such as this twelfth-century tower in Gaeta, Italy, evolved from the early defensive towers.

FIBONACCI MEASURES THE TOWER

The mathematician Leonardo Fibonacci is the most famous native of Pisa, second only to Galileo. His date of birth is uncertain, but apparently he was born shortly before construction began on the tower. As a young man, Fibonacci traveled widely, learning complex algebra and theories about mathematics. His fame as a mathematician spread throughout Italy and Europe as he developed what is today called the Fibonacci series. A simple example would be a series of numbers in which each number is the square of the preceding number, such as *2, 4, 16, 256,* and *65,536.*

Scholars who have studied the dimensions of the Tower of Pisa have come across evidence that perhaps Fibonacci's mathematics was used to determine the height of the tower as well as all other dimensions. Since neither the metric system nor the English system of feet and inches had yet to be invented, Pisans used a system of Fibonacci units today called Fibonacci arms and Fibonacci feet, which are roughly equal to the lengths of an average person's arm and foot.

Mathematicians who have measured the tower have found that the height of the tower, 193 feet, is equal to 100 Fibonacci arms, and its circumference at the base, 178 feet, is exactly 100 Fibonacci feet. To mathematicians familiar with Fibonacci's number sequencing, these measurements seem intentional, not coincidental.

These same mathematicians then began measuring other prominent elements of the tower to see if they might find more evidence of Fibonacci's number series. The measurements of the columns of the first open gallery are 9.5 feet tall, corresponding to 5 Fibonacci arms, and the height of each open gallery is exactly equal to two columns, or 10 Fibonacci arms. The mathematicians then discovered that if they multiplied these 10 Fibonacci arms times the six open galleries, the total was 60 Fibonacci arms, to which they added the double height of the base cylinder—20 Fibonacci arms and the 20 Fibonacci arms of the belfry for a grand total for all eight stories of again, 100 Fibonacci arms.

This careful analysis of the measurements of the tower indicates to mathematicians that the horizontal measurements were taken in Fibonacci feet and the vertical ones in Fibonacci arms.

medieval artists designed the exterior decorations to ensure that they would match a city's surrounding architecture.

In Pisa, the prevailing Romanesque style of architecture was first dictated by the building of the great cathedral to celebrate the city's defeat of its rival city, Palermo, in 1062. Begun in 1063 by the master builder Buschetto, the cathedral was consecrated in 1118, even though it was still years away from its completion date in the thirteenth century. Following the cathedral, Pisa built the baptistery that was used for the Christian ritual of baptism. Like the cathedral, it reflects Pisan Romanesque architectural characteristics, including a vast scale, the use of many delicate arches and columns, the lavish use of marble often highlighted with a second color, and tall, ornate colonnades set one above the other.

Having thus established the design standards for the city, architects and engineers determined long before the bell tower's construction began that its look would be consistent with those of the cathedral and baptistery. The tower must have seemed like a fairly straightforward project at the start of construction. What its builders could not possibly have foreseen was the flaw that would eventually bring more fame to the city of Pisa than any of its architectural treasures.

3

INITIAL
CONSTRUCTION
PHASE

In 1173 the builders commenced work on the Campanile di Pisa, Italian for the "Bell Tower of Pisa," or the Torre di Pisa, the "Tower of Pisa." Anticipation of the third successful major building in the Piazza dei Miracoli was palpable. Success must have seemed assured as the first shovelfuls of earth were extracted for Pisa's final monumental statement of civic pride.

THE DESIGN

To be consistent with the Pisan Romanesque style of the existing cathedral and baptistery, the tower would have multiple tiers of open colonnades—covered walkways supported by a series of columns reminiscent of the columns of ancient Roman design. It would also have extensive application of the white exterior marble that already graced the two existing buildings in the plaza.

The most obvious design characteristic of the Tower of Pisa is its cylindrical shape. Although most of the great bell towers in northern Italy, such as those of Venice and Florence, had square or rectangular bases, the Pisans wanted something more unusual to advertise their city. They also wanted a tower of unique beauty and elegance, something more elaborate than the earlier towers, which had been built of bland stone and were used against invading enemies. The new tower's regal exterior would express to all visitors the newfound wealth and power of this maritime trading center. No one could possibly confuse this wedding-cake design for a heavily fortified tower built to repel enemy armies.

The exterior of the tower achieved these goals with eight distinctive levels and colonnades supported by hundreds of delicate

47

marble columns that ring the perimeter. Because the outer wall lacks exterior openings or windows, it provides no clues whatsoever as to the interior nor how visitors find their way to the top. The tower actually has a hollow center core, similar to a stack of doughnuts, running from the ground to the belfry. Designers pro-

The builders of the Tower of Pisa wanted its exterior to exemplify the wealth of the city.

A staircase built within the walls of the Tower of Pisa spirals to the top of the structure.

vided access to the top by way of a narrow stone staircase spiraling up within the tower's thick cylindrical wall.

The bell tower is divided into three distinct elements: the ground floor, six levels of open galleries, and the belfry. The ground floor consists of a massive wall with exterior arches resting on fifteen marble pilasters. Above this ground level are stacked six more stories that are basically identical, with colonnades running around the exterior circumference, each having thirty full columns set eight feet out from the wall. The eighth and smallest story in diameter is the belfry, which houses the tower bells.

The cylindrical design of this eight-story bell tower is perfectly symmetrical. This means that if it were possible to slice it exactly down the middle, top to bottom, each of the two pieces would be identical. This symmetry would continue regardless of the number of times the tower was bisected.

Why is the tower eight stories as opposed to seven or nine or any other number? Notes written by the architect, Pisano, might allow modern art historians to answer this question. Unfortunately, none has survived. But professor David Speiser believes that the answer rests with the mythical story of the Tower of Babel mentioned in the Bible and he makes this observation:

> Of course the tower of Babel [is] the often reproduced and celebrated example of a high building. And what was known of it? The Bible does not tell us much, it speaks only of its destruction. But the more informative Herodotus [an ancient Greek historian] states explicitly that it had eight levels. In the first book of his history he writes: . . . "In the center of his sanctuary there is built a massive tower, one stadium long [two hundred feet] as well as large; upon this tower there is built another tower; upon this another one and so until the eighth one."[6]

Whatever the reason for the eight levels, the completion of the design stage of the tower allowed Pisano and the builders to move into the building stage. The building stage would require the work of engineers, common laborers, and artisans of many types to implement the design. The first workers would be the engineers familiar with foundation design and the laborers who would excavate the soil.

PHASE ONE: 1173–1178

The builders knew that the soil of the Piazza dei Miracoli contained more moisture than the soil in other districts of the city, but they believed this variation was to be expected in a city built along the banks of the Arno River so close to the sea. Besides, the cathedral and the baptistery stood firm, so why should they have any reason to be concerned with the location of this newest building?

What the twelfth-century Pisan builders could not know— and what modern engineers have determined—is that the changing course of the Arno River deposited a greater concentration of soft silt at the site of the bell tower than at the sites of the cathedral and the baptistery. The soil under the bell tower remained unusually moist due to small underground tributaries that continue to flow far below the surface.

Piero Pierotti, a member of the Commission for the Restoration of the Tower and a professor of medieval architecture at the University of Pisa, makes this comment about the foundation soil: "The layers of earth on which the bell-tower is constructed had different characteristics; the surface is accumulated fluvium [river mud] from the River Arno, while underneath there is a resistant layer of clay, with fine sand and salt [water] fish shells."[7]

An understanding of the soil beneath the tower is crucial for an understanding of its famous tilt. The first 23 feet consist of a mixture of mud and clay deposited by the Arno River and its many small tributaries. Between about 23 and 65 feet down, modern engineers who bored exploratory holes found a layer called Pancone clay that is made of flat, jumbled, loosely packed particles easily compressible. Below that, to a depth of 225 feet, are alternating layers of compacted sand, bedrock, and more clay. Unlike the compacted sand and bedrock at very deep levels,

The first 23 feet of soil beneath the Tower of Pisa consist of a mixture of mud and clay deposited by the Arno River (pictured) and its tributaries.

the layers closer to the surface lacked the compaction to support any heavy structure such as the bell tower. In fact, the composition of the soil layers was the worst possible that Pisano could have encountered for his massive design.

DIGGING THE FOUNDATION DITCH

Unfortunately, the builders were blissfully unaware of this fact as they began work. They started with the building's foundation, which had to be strong enough to support the massive downward pressure of the tower's weight—roughly 14,500 tons.

The first task was to establish the outline of the trench that would hold the foundation. Since the design for the tower was a cylinder with a hollow center, the foundation would be in the shape of a doughnut. For most square or rectangular towers, strings were stretched and attached to wooden stakes at each corner to define the outline of the trench. For this doughnut-shaped design, however, the center of the tower was marked by a large wooden stake driven into the ground. Then two strings were attached to this center stake, one the length of the outer radius of the circle and the other the length of the inner radius. Stretching the two strings taut and tying a chisel to each end, surveyors walked the circle scraping a deep line in the dirt that would be the outline for the trenchers. When the entire outline was completed, trenchers began the tedious task of digging the foundation trench into which the concrete would later be poured.

Digging the trench was hard physical work that required the age-old rudimentary tools of picks, shovels, wicker baskets, wheelbarrows, and bare hands. The master builder supervised the work, checking all dimensions and paying particular attention to the depth and any evidence of groundwater. If too much water were found, workers would either need to drain the area, firm it up with wooden pilings tipped with iron and driven deep into the clay, or add a thick layer of gravel. When the trenchers had reached the desired depth, surveyors checked the trench to make sure the base was perfectly level. To accomplish this, they used a water level that has a history of use as far back as the Greeks and Egyptians.

STABILIZING THE SOIL

The inner diameter of the finished trench was 24.5 feet and the outer diameter was 63.5 feet, creating a 39-foot-wide circular

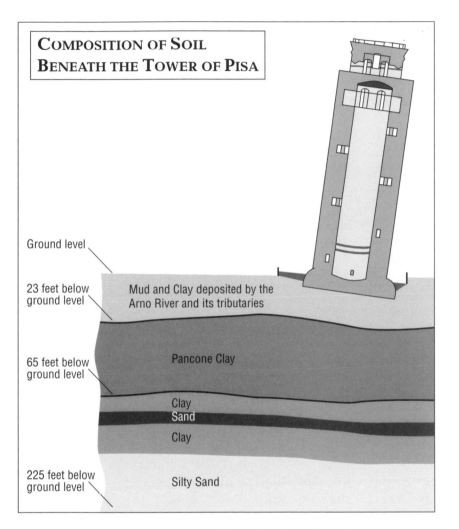

COMPOSITION OF SOIL BENEATH THE TOWER OF PISA

Ground level

23 feet below ground level — Mud and Clay deposited by the Arno River and its tributaries

65 feet below ground level — Pancone Clay

Clay
Sand
Clay

225 feet below ground level — Silty Sand

ditch to a depth of 10 feet. After having dug the enormous trench, medieval engineers needed to make a decision regarding the ability of the soil to support the tower. This was the time to stabilize the soil if it seemed too moist and loose. Once the concrete foundation was poured, it would be too late. Engineers in other northern Italian cities had from time to time attempted to solidify soft soil using wooden pilings driven deep into the spongy clay. This type of soil preparation was used with considerable success under palaces in the city of Venice, where the soil was far more saturated than in Pisa.

The engineers working on the tower decided they would need some sort of support. Instead of wooden pilings, however, they applied a sixteen-inch layer of crushed gravel similar to that used to secure modern railroad tracks. Although they believed that this depth would be sufficient, it was woefully insufficient for the tremendous weight. Several feet would have been the more prudent decision. But medieval engineers had not yet discovered the mathematics that modern engineers use when faced with these sorts of decisions involving downward pressures and the soil's ability to distribute and to resist them.

So far as Pisano was concerned, the one last element needed before the concrete pour was the wooden form. The purpose of the wooden form that was placed inside the trench was to contain and shape the concrete foundation beneath the soil to the exact engineering specifications. Trenches were always dug much wider than necessary because digging tools were imprecise. Early primitive foundations were poured directly into the trench, but when dealing with a large, complicated tower, a more precise concrete foundation was required.

FORMING AND POURING THE FOUNDATION

Carpenters began building wooden forms after the trench had been completed. The wooden forms were made of long planks nailed to stakes that were driven into the bottom of the trench. Since the walls of the first floor would be thirteen feet thick, the concrete foundation had to be twice the thickness of the walls, or twenty-six feet wide. The two circular parallel form walls were set exactly twenty-six feet apart within the trench. After inspectors confirmed that the distance between the two sides was exactly the same all the way around, the outsides of the forms were backfilled with dirt to help contain the inside pressure once the dense concrete was added.

Thousands of wagons of concrete were mixed and poured into the enormous form. The pour went on without interruption until the form was filled to the top. The composition of the concrete was nearly identical to that first discovered by the Romans during the first century B.C. Medieval builders understood its unique quality of flowing like a liquid when wet and conforming to the shape of the forms when hard.

Masons removed the wooden forms after the concrete footing had hardened for several weeks. The tower was now ready for the next phase of building—the first floor. From this point upward, all floors of the tower would be above ground and most of their architectural elements would be visible to the citizens of Pisa.

THE FIRST FLOOR

After digging the foundation ditch, building the form, and pouring the concrete foundation, masons started to erect the wall of the ground floor. This 13-foot-thick wall would need to be thick enough to transfer to the concrete foundation the entire weight of the tower as it rose to its final height of 193 feet. The first-story wall sits directly on top of, and in the center of, the 26-foot-thick concrete foundation.

The wall is so precisely constructed that it is impossible to tell simply by looking at it how it was built or of what material it was built. In fact, the outer edges of the wall consist of heavy stone blocks

Blind arches embellished with diamond-shaped insets called coffers decorate the Tower of Pisa's first floor.

cemented together. The medieval Pisan designers, always mindful of the aesthetics of the tower, then covered the one edge visible to the public with one-foot-thick blocks of multicolored marble. Masons responsible for cutting these heavy marble blocks did so with such precision that the space between them is less than the thickness of a credit card. Although this marble was added to beautify the wall, it also provided additional strength. The edge of the wall not visible to the public was left plain.

The area in between the two edges was filled with concrete instead of stone blocks. Using concrete was a cost-saving technique because it did not involve the labor costs of carting large stones to the construction site, hand cutting each block, and then hoisting and cementing thousands of them in place. But before the builders could fill the space between the two edges with concrete, they first had to build a forty-inch-wide spiraling staircase in this space.

Since this staircase would be the only one in the tower and could not be located anywhere else, builders first built the staircase and then filled in the remaining space with concrete. Ultimately, the decision to place a staircase in the middle of the wall would prove problematic because its presence decreased the amount of concrete in the wall, thereby reducing the wall's strength.

MARBLE DECORATIONS

The wall and staircase were never decorated because they were hidden in the tower's interior. Its exterior, however, would be seen by everyone and so required elaborate decorations. The exterior of the ground floor has a look very different from the floors that rise above it. The tower's architect, Pisano, knew that visitors and citizens strolling around the grounds of the Piazza dei Miracoli would be able to see details on the first floor better than on the higher ones. Wishing to create a decorative motif that would match the ornateness of the existing cathedral and baptistery within the plaza, Pisano designed a perfect addition to the other two grand examples of Pisan Romanesque architecture.

Pisano designed a marble colonnade that ran the entire circumference of the first floor, and consisted of fifteen marble Corinthian pilasters set directly against the exterior wall. Above and between every two pilasters Pisano set a decorative blind arch that sprang from one of the pilasters to the next. Within each blind arch he placed a decorative motif called a coffer— that is, an inset diamond shape with a sculpted flower in the center. The visual effect of all of this marble is stunning because intermingled with the white Carrara marble are striking highlights of green Verdi marble, providing a two-tone color scheme. For Pisans out for a walk, this first floor must have been a visual delight and a source of civic pride.

The ground floor stands thirty-six feet high. Here, visitors find the only entry to the tower. Pisano had gained early renown in Pisa as the sculptor of the bronze doors for Pisa's cathedral. In keeping with this fame, he built a bronze double-door entryway for the tower. Remarkably simple, these two matching doors have three raised panels each but no decorative sculpture.

The only other two openings on this first floor are two narrow windows to the left of the doors. Both are too narrow to allow entry, and at just eight inches wide, neither allows much light into the empty interior core of the tower. One might think that Pisano would have spaced windows evenly around the base

These bronze double doors provide the only entrance into the Tower of Pisa.

of the tower to maintain the symmetry of the design, but he did not. Not only are these two existing windows not evenly distributed, but they are not even the same size. The larger of the two is centered between the ground and the top of the first floor, but the smaller one is closer to the top of the floor than to the ground. These two windows are so small that it is hard to believe that they could possibly have had much value.

Pisano placed on the wall, just to the right of the bronze doors, a sculpted relief representing a bull and a bear that is biting a dragon's tail. Various art historians see this as representing the struggle between the devil (the dragon), tempting humanity (the bull), and the divine grace (the bear). Directly under this sculpted relief appears a Latin inscription that is the only document that historians have found regarding the tower. It reads, "ANNO DOMMINI

Some historians believe that this engraving of two ships and a tower, located to the right of the Tower of Pisa's bronze doors, represents the church leading Christians' souls into the port of salvation.

MCLXXIIII CAMPANILE HOC FUIT FUNDATUM MENSE AUGUSTI," which means, "The foundation of this bell tower was laid in the month of August A.D. 1174."

Although the Roman numerals in the inscription specify a date of 1174, Pierotti, explains that the dating system at that time was off by one year and that the official date for setting the first stone was, in fact, August 9, 1173.

A little bit higher on the same wall, Pisano placed a second sculpted relief representing a tower in the middle of the sea with two ships at its sides. Art historians believe that this figure either signifies the church leading Christians' souls into the port of salvation or represents the old harbor of Pisa when the sea came closer to the city's center.

To the left of the double doors are fragments of a funereal inscription for Bonanno Pisano, obviously placed here at a much later date. Apparently his white marble funeral urn was entombed somewhere within the tower and was accidentally exhumed in 1820. Translated into English, the Latin inscription reads, "Fragments of a sepulchral inscription bearing the name of Bonanno of Pisa, builder, of this marvelous edifice were accidentally exhumed in 1820. With great care, they were returned at a memorial service for the great architect in February of 1841."[8]

To the right, just in front of this urn, is a large memorial stone that was set on the occasion of the First Congress of the Scientists held in Pisa in 1839. This gathering paid tribute to the city's most famous native, the scientist Galileo Galilei. Translated, the Latin inscription reads,

> Galileo Galilei, while performing experiments from the top of this Leaning Tower on the fall of heavy bodies discovered the laws of movement, founded mechanics that surpassed his own great discoveries and those of his successors. As a memorial to his work, Vincenzo Carmignani Operajo . . . dedicated this grave stone on the 1st of October 1839.[9]

No additional inscriptions or sculptures are found above the first floor.

THE SECOND AND THIRD FLOORS

Following the completion of the foundation and the first floor, Pisano and his master builder moved on to the middle six floors, whose height and external decorations would be identical to each other yet very different from the first floor.

Though not as tall as the first floor, each of the six center floors provided an 18-foot-tall, 360-degree colonnade that visitors could stroll around. As visitors ascended the interior staircase, they could exit onto any of the six floors to take in the view of the Piazza dei Miracoli, located directly adjacent to the tower below, or a view of the entire city.

Beginning with the second floor, the thickness of the circular wall decreased from 13 feet on the first floor to 8.5 feet to make room for the colonnades. This 4.5-foot reduction in thickness reduced the wall's ability to support the tower, particularly since 40 inches of the wall's remaining girth was not solid but was taken up by the spiraling stone staircase located within the wall.

The colonnade extended about eight feet out from the wall to the thirty marble columns that supported its outer edge. Remarkably, no safety rail was ever provided, making the breathtaking view considerably dangerous for the foolhardy. As on the first floor, the cylinder wall for these floors was covered with elegant marble blocks to delight Pisan eyes.

The thirty marble columns that support the outer lip of each floor were decorated with capitals carved with scrolls at the

GALILEO AND GRAVITY

Galileo Galilei, the most famous astronomer of the Renaissance, was born in Pisa in 1564. He received his early education there, until he moved to Florence in 1575. He studied at a monastery until 1581, when he returned home to Pisa to study at University of Pisa to become a doctor. Galileo was attracted to mathematics rather than medicine, and he also began to take an interest in physics. In about 1583 he discovered that a pendulum always swings back and forth with the same frequency, regardless of the length of the swing. He made this discovery while attending a church service in Pisa's cathedral by using his pulse to time the swing of several candelabras on different lengths of chain.

In 1589 Galileo became professor of mathematics at the University of Pisa. He attacked the theories of the Greek philosopher Aristotle, who believed that objects of different weights fall at different speeds. To disprove Aristotle's theory, Galileo proposed an experiment.

To perform this experiment, he needed the tallest tower he could find. In Pisa, it was, of course, the Leaning Tower. Galileo sent one of his students to the top of the tower with two cannon balls of different weights. At a signal, the student dropped the two cannon balls at precisely the same time. As Galileo predicted, the two struck the ground at the same time, proving that all objects fall at the same rate. He published his first ideas on motion in his publication *De Motu*, Latin for *About Motion*, in 1590.

Galileo Galilei, the most famous astronomer of the Renaissance.

Colonnades extend eight feet from the Tower of Pisa's walls, providing visitors with a breathtaking view of the Piazza dei Miracoli.

corners that identify them as Ionic capitals, unlike the Corinthian capitals found on the ground level. As on the first floor, a beautiful arch carved in marble springs from Ionic capital to Ionic capital. At the springing of each arch directly above each Ionic capital, pieces of inlaid green and white marble cut in triangular shapes were cemented in place as an elegant decorative detail. This motif is repeated on each of the thirty arches on each of the six middle floors.

SOMETHING AMISS

With the completion of the second floor and work pressing along on schedule for the third, casual visitors stopping by to see the progress marveled at the beautiful design and the marble stonework. Most probably failed to see what had caught the eye of supervisors making their daily site visits. As the tower went up, a

The columns of every floor except for the ground floor of the Tower of Pisa are decorated with Ionic capitals.

significant percentage of its eventual total weight was now pressing down on the foundation poured ten feet below ground level. What had attracted the supervisors' attention, one by one, was a minute lean on the north side of the tower. The base that had been at ground level was ever so slightly disappearing below the turf.

Such a lean was not uncommon. Experienced builders had seen them before and usually, after a while, the lean either stopped or the entire structure eventually leveled out. For the moment, no one panicked as the third floor was well under way and the citizens of Pisa eagerly awaited the completion of their prized beauty.

As the third floor neared completion in 1178, the tilting of the north side was not only not subsiding, but it was also becoming increasingly apparent to the work crews. Correcting a sinking foundation would be impossible at this point. As an alternative, masons tried to level the third floor by cutting the stone on the north side slightly longer than on the south side to compensate for the slight lean. Leveling the tower part way up was more likely to solve the problem since jacking up the sinking side was not an option this late in construction. Two modern professors at the University of Pisa, Francesco Gambino and Fiorella Morabito believe that the northern tilt of the tower at this point in construction was about two inches off vertical.

Although no records exist of meetings between the builders and the town council paying for the tower, it is easy to imagine the agitation and disappointment expressed by both sides. In 1178 the project was abandoned, leaving the seventy-two-foot tall, partially completed tower to languish for the next ninety-four years. Historians in two disputing camps offer two possible explanations for the work stoppage, one of which focuses on the problems with the tower and one that does not.

One group of historians believes that construction ceased to allow the tower to complete its settling before finishing it. Indeed, several structural engineers have expressed the view that had the postponement not occurred, it is highly likely that the tower would have toppled. John Burland, a modern geologist and a member of the Pisa Commission, a group of scientists investigating the tower's dilemma, takes this view:

> If they'd built the Tower in one go, it literally would have fallen over . . . that's what would have happened if they'd built it all in one shot. So what they actually did was, they built the Tower up to a little above the third story and then they stopped. And the weight of that Tower in that state squeezed the underlying ground, and over the years the ground became stronger. So when they came back 100 years later it could take the full weight of the Tower.[10]

The other camp believes that the many wars that Pisa fought against Florence consumed all of the city's financial resources, forcing the civic leaders to send all of the workers home. Although historians debate this cessation, the majority believes that a war with Florence is the most likely explanation.

4

FINAL CONSTRUCTION PHASE

As the war tightened its grip on the city, the money and energy needed to keep the tower construction going went for cannons and gunpowder instead. Lost to the city after five years of work were the sights, sounds, and smells of the construction work that had poured over the site, gradually lifting a stunningly beautiful work of art out of the mud and clay.

Although there is no surviving documentation describing the actual construction of the Tower of Pisa, many histories and drawings of other major twelfth- and thirteenth-century Romanesque buildings tell the story. Major architectural undertakings today attract the attention of many citizens and the same was true in Pisa and other leading cultural centers throughout Europe.

The construction site came to life at sunrise as the craftsmen left their crude straw and stick shacks located at the base of the tower, where they lived as long as they worked on the project. These shantytowns were a common sight on construction sites and housed the many members of the work crew who traveled from city to city performing their craft without a permanent home of their own. Experienced craftsmen were difficult to find, and cities were willing to pay handsomely for their expertise.

The person with the highest status on the work site was not the lead architect but rather the master builder. The names of the master builders of majestic structures were well-known in medieval times. Cities willing to spend huge sums of money to enhance their civic position and reputation would trust these high-profile structures only to well-seasoned builders who understood the complexities of large-scale construction. Besides being the most respected man on the site, the master builder was also the best paid.

Final responsibility for all work on the tower fell to the master builder, who coordinated and controlled all building activities. He moved the project forward as quickly as possible by hiring and firing workers, ordering materials, purchasing all large tools for the job, and keeping several crews working in harmony on a full-time basis. When a piece of work was completed, it was also his responsibility to inspect it to ensure the highest possible quality for a tower intended to win fame and prestige for the city paying the hefty price tag.

Implementing the architectural drawings was also the master builder's responsibility. He would walk about the construction site barking orders to the different crews and checking work for accuracy. Drafted on parchment—the cleaned skins of goats, sheep, and calves—the architectural drawings were

The master builder oversaw all aspects of a building's construction.

drawn to scale to depict the precise height, length, and width of foundations, rooms, and staircases. Additional sheets of parchment detailed such things as roof design, sculptural details, and the placement of doors and windows. Because the plans were one-of-a-kind and expensive to produce, the master builder carefully guarded them. When the plans were no longer needed, the skins were scraped clean and reused. Over time, the parch-

Stonemasons employed a variety of tools to construct the Tower of Pisa's masonry.

ment either wore out or became dry and brittle, eventually deteriorating to dust.

Several teams of support craftsmen set up shop as close to the tower as possible to assist the masons and carpenters. Stonemasons needed picks, hammers, wedges, hatchets, spades, chisels, trowels, hoes, buckets, and sieves to accomplish their work. Accompanying any work crew was the blacksmith's shop, with its hot fire for heating iron and anvil to hammer repairs, sharpen edges, repair chisel points, and craft iron tools needed for stonework. Carpenters also had their shop equipped with two-man saws for cutting and hewing the heavy beams for scaffolding and roof beams as well as providing all wood for concrete forms. All of these cutting tools needed frequent sharpening or replacement, and an entire industry existed at a construction site to keep everyone productively working.

When the war with Florence came to an end, Pisan officials announced their intent to continue work on the partially completed tower. It would take several weeks to hire a new master builder and a work crew to move forward with the tower.

PHASE TWO: 1272–1278

In 1272 the decision to resume construction on the bell tower sent an entirely new team of builders back to Pisa to complete the city's jewel. The war had silenced the construction site for ninety-four years. Four generations of Pisans had been born, lived their lives, and died knowing the bell tower as an elaborate three-story marble stump from which the chiming of bells had never been heard.

Since not so much as a single block of stone had been set in nearly one hundred years, the first order of business was the acquisition of more building materials. The job of providing the immense quantity of marble and building stone needed for the tower was costly and difficult. The biggest expense was the cost of carting the heavy marble stones from quarries throughout Italy to Pisa. An ox-pulled wagon was the most efficient way to accomplish this backbreaking job. Sometimes, however, peasants were hitched to wagons and made to pull them in return for a minimal amount of money.

THE STONE WORK

The job of shaping chunks of marble into the beautiful columns that still stand on the tower today was done with a machine tool

A modern quarryman watches as oxen transport blocks of marble from an Italian quarry. Oxen-pulled wagons were also used to transport the heavy marble stones needed for the construction of the Tower of Pisa.

called a lathe. A rectangular piece of marble was placed horizontally across the lathe and was spun as fast as possible. The spinning was accomplished either by foot on a treadle or by a hand crank. Spinning the lathe as fast as they could, the masons moved their chisels back and forth across the length of the spinning marble column on a guide, gradually removing even amounts of marble until the columns reached the desired diameter.

Large columns, like those found in the cathedral, were too heavy for hand-turned lathes. Instead, they were built from a series of drums, three to four feet tall, stacked one on top of the other like poker chips. Once the drums were cemented in place, sculptors would chisel them into the desired shape. This process was much slower and more expensive than shaping small columns on a lathe.

As marble colonnades and block walls climbed higher, workmen needed scaffolding to stand on in order to raise the walls and to heft their construction materials to greater heights.

SCAFFOLDING

The age-old technique of building temporary platforms on which workers could stand has changed little over the past three thousand years. Dominating the tower's construction sites was the external skeleton of roughly cut low-grade wooden poles and planks growing from the ground floor eventually all the way up to the belfry. Two distinct types of scaffolding were used: one freestanding and the other attached to the walls.

Freestanding scaffolding was built from the ground up on long poles set vertically on the ground every ten feet around the tower. Two circles of these poles were necessary to support cross planking, on which the workers stood above the ground. The planking, lashed to the poles with strips of leather, was given additional strength with diagonal poles held tight by leather tourniquets. As the walls went higher and higher, more poles were secured to the lower ones, and this process of stacking continued until the scaffolding reached the top of the tower.

Early scaffolding is depicted on this thirteenth-century wall mosaic of the Tower of Babel's construction.

Scaffolding attached directly to the walls followed a very different principle than the freestanding type. Long, heavy timbers, eight to ten inches thick and between twenty and thirty feet long, were inserted through holes in the wall with eight to ten feet extending out beyond both sides of the wall. Because the protruding sections were balanced by the width of the wall, workmen could lay heavy planking across them to create a secure working platform along the wall. As workers filled the area between the two walls with concrete, the dense wet concrete added to the stability of the timbers. When the process of setting the timbers and pouring the concrete was done properly, workers were able to extract the timbers before the concrete hardened around them for reuse at the next highest level. When the beams were extracted, a hole the thickness of the beam was left behind to be patched with concrete at a later time. Sometimes, however, the process did not proceed correctly and the timbers became forever imprisoned in the walls. Carpenters then cut off the length extending beyond the walls. The problem with leaving the timbers in the walls was that, as they decayed over time, they left behind weak spots that compromised the integrity of the walls.

Cranes such as the ones shown in this sixteenth-century illustration of the rebuilding of Troy were used to lift heavy loads up to workers on scaffolding.

Whichever type of scaffolding was used, workmen scrambled up and down the tower daily to set stone, work on the roof, or attach ornamental stonework. The strength of the scaffolding was limited, and sometimes overly zealous work crews sent it crashing to the ground.

Lifting heavy loads up to the workers on the scaffolding was the job of cranes set on stone platforms inside the building. Each crane had a long, boom-like arm built of heavy timbers that dangled over the edge of the scaffolding. Attached to it was a rope that secured a load on the ground. At a signal, oxen were driven around in a circle, winding up the rope on a large wheel and sending the load upward to the workers on the scaffolding.

Now that the new work crews had arrived and the needed building materials were available, builders were ready to resume where their predecessors had left off.

A NEW LEAN

The tower greeted the new generation of builders with a tilt that their great-great-grandfathers would have found truly remarkable. The tower was no longer leaning to the north—it was now leaning to the south. For reasons probably unfathomable to these medieval craftsmen who knew nothing about geology or hydrology, the lean had not gone away but instead had rotated 180 degrees.

How could this reversal happen? Modern geologists believe that after the ground had frozen and thawed many times, the clay and silt below the south side of the tower began compressing at a much faster rate than the ground on the north side. To this occurrence was added the second phenomenon of compaction. As the tower was tipping slowly to the south, more of the weight came to rest on the south foundation, so that the soil on that side compacted even more than on the north side. These two phenomena set in motion a continuous cycle: The tower tipped, the soil compacted, the tower tipped more, the soil compacted more, and so forth.

Regardless of this odd phenomenon, work resumed to complete the remaining four center floors up to the belfry. Since these four floors would be identical to the previous two, the task of copying them was relatively simple. But what should be done about the lean to the south? It is highly likely that the new builders were aware that the third floor had been slightly lengthened on the north side to compensate for the northerly lean because that became the solution to the new problem of correcting the southerly lean.

BUILDING A BANANA: FLOORS FOUR THROUGH SEVEN

At this point, correcting the tower's lean became increasingly complicated. The initial lean to the north had been corrected, but now there was a more pronounced lean to the south, and the new builders had to correct for this new lean opposite the first one. As the next four floors went up, builders lengthened the walls and columns along the south side in an attempt to create the appearance of a perfectly straight tower. The workers put taller pieces of stone on the south side and shorter ones on the north. The engineering necessary to correct the different angles of lean caused the tower to arc much like the familiar curve of a banana.

In 1272 the architect working on these four floors, Giovanni di Simone, set about correcting the new lean by heightening the south side of the fourth floor 6.6 inches above the north side. As the fifth, sixth, and seventh floors took shape, di Simone found that these too needed corrections, which suggests that the tower continued to settle along the south side. Di Simone elevated the south side of the fifth floor an additional 1.5 inches, and as he completed the sixth and seventh floors, the tilt continued to worsen until 1278, when work on the tower once again stopped due to continuing wars with rival Italian trading centers.

Regardless of how hard di Simone tried to compensate for the continuing lean, he could not keep up with what must have seemed a problem without a solution. When construction temporarily stopped again, the tower tilted to the south roughly 2.5 feet. The lean was actually accelerating, and the plan to arch the tower back to a vertical position like a banana was failing to keep up.

PHASE THREE: 1360–1370

When construction resumed for the third time in 1360, eighty-two years later, and nearly two hundred years after Pisano had begun the tower, the lean had become still more pronounced. It now reached slightly more than four feet. Soil engineer John Burland reflects on the first and second postponements by observing that "in both cases the masons stopped just in the nick of time. Because they left it, the weight of the tower squeezed a lot of the water out of the clay, and the clay became stronger."[11]

An architect, who is unknown to history, finished the last floor and the belfry in 1370. He continued to try to curve the tower back to the centerline with one final sixteen-inch elevation of the south side over the north. Visitors to the belfry noticed that there were six steps from the lip of the seventh floor up to the belfry on the south side but only four steps on the north side.

THE BELFRY: FLOOR EIGHT

The design of this eighth and last floor was significantly different from the other seven because of its function as a belfry. Although it is the same height as the ground floor, thirty-six feet, the tower has no roof whatsoever. The tower was designed to emit the sounds of bells, and the open roof maximizes the distance that the bells' tones carry. The walls of the eighth floor also lack the colonnades found on the six middle floors, which allowed visitors to walk around the tower. Instead, six large open arches, alternating with six small ones, pierce the circular wall. The large arches begin at floor level and arc halfway up the wall, much like a door, while the small arches are more like windows because their bases begin halfway up the wall and arc close to the top of the wall. Unlike the blind arches on the first floor, these six large and six small open arches extend all the way through the walls. The bells hang on wooden timbers within these arches. As they rang out, their sounds emanated 360 degrees for miles across the Pisan landscape.

The Tower of Pisa's belfry was designed without a roof to allow the bells' tones to carry great distances.

Two decorative architectural elements complete the belfry. Next to each large arch stand two marble pilasters. This total of twelve is similar to the marble pilasters on the first floor. Half are sculpted in the Corinthian order with acanthus leaves, and six are Ionic with the traditional scrollwork that is also found on the middle six floors. Above each of the six large arches is set two blind arches side by side. The tops of the blind arches align with the tops of the small open arches to form a continuous band around the top of the tower.

The bells of the Tower of Pisa hang from wooden timbers placed within the open arches of the belfry.

As the tower neared completion, bell makers began work on what Pisano thought would be the tower's most famous feature. Each of the original bells has its own name and story. The oldest is called Pasquereccia. According to the Latin inscription it bears, it was cast in 1262 by a Pisan bell maker named Lotteringo and was paid for by a patron named Gerardo. The inscription is decorated with small roses, a winged lion, an eagle, a winged horse, and an angel. This particular bell was rung whenever a criminal or traitor was beheaded. The most modern bell is named the Crocefisso ("Crucifix") and was cast in 1818 by a man named Gualandi from the city of Prato.

The biggest bell is called Assunta because it is decorated with a low relief sculpture of the ascent of the Virgin Mary. Cast in 1655 by Pietro Orlando, it weighs 3.6 tons. On the north side there is a bell called the Vespruccio because it is rung during Vespers, or evening prayers, at about six P.M.

In addition to these more well-known bells, there was also Saint Ranieri's bell, dedicated to the patron saint of the town, which was cast by Berti of Lucca in 1735; Pozzo's bell, which was paid for by Archbishop Pozzo in 1616; and the Terza, or three o'clock, bell, which was cast in 1474 and was so named because it was the custom to ring it at that hour.

SIGNS OF DESPAIR

What had to have been a bitter disappointment to the people of Pisa during the tower's construction quickly turned to despair. Only a few years after the tower's completion, cracks began to appear in the stone wall and marble columns. Of greater concern than the cracks, however, were marble chips found scattered about some of the floors. This structural damage was further evidence of problems caused by the lean, and for the first time engineers inspecting the tower expressed concern about its structural integrity.

Documentation indicates that in 1398 marble was purchased to replace broken pieces along the south wall. More restoration was carried out later, including the replacement of fifty cracked marble columns from several of the floors during the 1500s. These columns, which had originally been made of marble quarried at San Guiliano, were replaced with columns made from marble from the quarries of Carrara. Marble from Carrara was chosen because it was cheaper than San Guiliano marble.

SHELLING THE TOWER

Few people are aware that during World War II the Leaning Tower of Pisa was nearly destroyed during the German retreat from Italy in 1944. As the American and British armies drove north and the German army fled the country, many towns, including Pisa, became battlegrounds.

When the U.S. Army reached Pisa, Sergeant Leon Weckstein was ordered by his commander to get as close as he could to the tower because the Germans were using it as an observation post. The idea was to radio its position to a U.S. Navy cruiser positioned just off the coast that would then shell the tower with its heavy guns.

Hiding in an olive grove, the sergeant scanned the tower with his binoculars but could not make out the presence of Germans on the tower, although it was the most obvious place for them to be. After several hours, heavy German bombardments forced Weckstein to retreat without issuing the order to shell the famous tower.

He later told his commanders that the last thing he wanted to do was to be the man who called in the artillery strike to the cruiser. His commanders, understanding his reluctance to destroy an eight hundred-year-old landmark, told him that they had decided in advance not to shell the tower, even if he had called the cruiser to do so.

By the time all replacements had been completed, 175 of the 207 column shafts had been substituted with white Carrara marble; likewise, 195 of the 207 capitals had also been substituted with Carrara marble.

This voluminous replacement was necessary because the tower's extreme tilt of twelve feet was compressing the tower, causing the pillars and other marble structural elements to buckle and crack. This tilt was described in a 1999 *NOVA* television broadcast:

The Tower has always been cared for by an organization called the Opera, whose presidents represent an unbroken line of craftsmen right back to the 11th century. The Opera archives contain a priceless hoard of information.

A report from 1550 showed the top was already 12 feet south of the base.[12]

In spite of the restoration and replacement of marble, the decay continued. More was going wrong than just the lean. Any marble building exposed to the sun, wind, and rain will sustain damage. Although marble is a form of stone, it is not one of the harder ones such as granite. Natural stresses on marble can cause its crystal structure to decompose to a fine, sandy powder, reducing its volume and strength. As a secondary effect of the marble's decomposition and weakening, the joints between the marble elements of the tower began to pull apart, causing pieces to collapse or to become unreliable in even a small earthquake. To try to hold the marble elements together, engineers applied iron rings, brackets, and chains to support numerous areas of the tower.

Besides the damage caused by the elements, there was still the problem of excessive moisture in the subsoil and even, from time to time, small rivulets flowing sporadically at the base of the tower. As a testimony to the never-ending problems caused by the soft, wet subsoil in the Piazza dei Miracoli, in the year 1650, not far from the Leaning Tower, a concrete-and-marble water fountain sank out of sight below ground level for the second time.

For dozens of generations, Pisans lived with the dilemma of a significant Romanesque edifice poised on the brink of collapse. The citizens there recognized its value as a tourist attraction, funneling millions of dollars into the city's treasury, but they also recognized that its lean might soon cause it to fall with disastrous consequences. Although many civic groups had met to discuss a remedy to the tilt, none had found a solution. Something more significant needed to be done before it was too late.

5

MODERN
RESTORATION

Concern over the one great flaw in the Tower of Pisa has over-shadowed all of its architectural characteristics. Although art historians as well as casual tourists have praised the tower's Romanesque elegance, the fear of its collapse has always eclipsed its architectural fame, as is suggested in the following overview of the tower:

> In the 12th century, in a Europe ravaged by war, famine and disease, the rich Italian city of Pisa rose above the horror by erecting the most magnificent Tower the world had ever seen. 800 years later this bold architectural dream has produced a nightmare. Inch by inch, year by year, the Tower is slowly tipping over. What was once an amusing tourist attraction is now a threat. The top hangs 17 feet south of the base—and the Leaning Tower of Pisa is on the brink of disaster.[13]

In 1909 the first of what would eventually be seventeen Pisa commissions was appointed to study and follow the changing conditions of the tower. At this time it was affirmed that the tower's lean was 13.5 feet and that the lean had increased by over 10 inches since the last reliable measurement in 1817 by an English team of researchers. The commission also concluded that a small underground spring that was carrying off soil was undermining the tower at its base, increasing the lean by about .04 inches per year.

In 1933, after many years of careful research, a remedy was suggested to divert the underground spring. The idea was to inject concrete through 361 holes, two inches in diameter, under the tower's base, making the foundation watertight. Work was completed following the injection of over one hundred tons of concrete, at which time engineers installed a more accurate plumb line to measure the tower's movement.

The effects of fooling around with the foundation were disastrous. The new plumb line recorded a southward lurch of nearly a tenth of an inch. The work had destabilized the delicate tower. These became times of desperation, as engineers were willing to try anything to stop the continuing tilt. In the 1950s, the commission locked down all seven bells, fearing that their swinging might contribute to the tower's fall.

A TICKING TIME BOMB

From the very beginning, when Pisano and his assistants first confronted the gut-wrenching reality that their tower was leaning, steps were taken to remedy the curse of the spongy subsoil on which the tower had been built. The one fact that has become indisputable after so many failed attempts to straighten the tower is that the soil under the foundation was never properly prepared to support the tremendous weight of the tower. All of the piecemeal attempts to correct the lean over the tower's eight-hundred-year history simply worsened an already difficult situation that was soon to turn desperate.

The city of Pavia, 120 miles north of Pisa, had been welcoming visitors who flocked there to climb the stairs to its fourteenth-century bell tower. In 1989, while hundreds of tourists made their way to the belfry, a shudder ran through the tower. Panic erupted as everyone fled the vibrating tower, believing they were in the midst of an earthquake. Tragically, they were not able to escape

The wreckage of the Pavia bell tower, which collapsed in 1989, lies next to the city's cathedral.

fast enough. The tower collapsed, crushing to death four visitors near the base. After the site was inspected, it was discovered that this tragedy had not been the result of an earthquake after all but rather extensive deterioration of the foundation and walls.

The news of the collapse of the tower at Pavia sent shock waves through Italy and especially through Pisa. Fearing what might happen if their own tower were to topple, Pisan city officials locked the tower's bronze doors for the first time on January 7, 1990, and placed a fence around it, closing it to all visitors.

TROUBLED TOWERS

The Tower of Pisa is not the only medieval tower in northern Italy to have experienced serious structural flaws. An investigation of many bell towers in this region indicated that many of them suffer from various types of geological and structural defects, which have damaged some and collapsed others. Pisa is by no means the only northern Italian town with a leaning tower. The cities of Modena and Bologna each have towers that are also leaning. These towers date from the same time as the one in Pisa and lean for the same reason: moist clay subsoil that caused them to settle at an angle.

The restoration effort at Pisa was prompted less by the accelerating lean that had been known for hundreds of years than by the collapse of the bell tower at Pavia, a town north of Pisa, whose tower crumbled to the ground, killing four persons in 1989. This tower, constructed very similarly to the tower in Pisa, was not even leaning. Its primary design flaw was the construction of walls that were strong along the outer edges but were very weak in the middle. This same flaw existed in the tower at Pisa, although it was secondary to the problem of the soft soil.

On July 14, 1902, another disastrous incident occurred in the internationally renowned city of Venice. The massive three-hundred-foot campanile in Saint Mark's Square, constructed over a 276-year period between 874 and 1150, suddenly collapsed. Although the tower was immediately rebuilt, engineers believe that the cause of the collapse was a restoration job at a nearby site, where

At this point city officials, urged on by the Italian government in Rome, designated the seventeenth Pisa Commission. Headed by structural engineer Michele Jamiolkowski, a professor at the Polytechnic University in Turin, Italy, and consisting of Italian and foreign experts in the fields of structural engineering, soil engineering, and restoration of monuments, the commission declared the tower to be on the verge of collapse.

The commission allocated a sizable amount of money to send this team of internationally renowned scientists scrambling for a solution. The first step would be to perform a thorough

The campanile in Saint Mark's Square in Venice was rebuilt after it suddenly collapsed in 1902.

construction workers unwittingly cut through a reinforcement wall that had been added to support the tower in the mid–eighteenth century after damage from lightning.

Earthquakes have also taken their toll in northern Italy. In September 1997 two earthquakes struck the region of Assisi, inflicting massive damage to several Romanesque structures, including the cathedral and small adjoining tower. It is now widely accepted that the worst damage was the result of a restoration of the roof thirty years ago, when the original timber supports were replaced by concrete ones. Since concrete is heavier and more rigid than wood, it is believed that the additional weight was too much for the walls and dome during the quake.

analysis of the tower—its condition, its history, and how to proceed with the best-possible remedy.

THE CURRENT CONDITION

The commission of scientists found themselves in a situation similar to that of an emergency-room staff at a modern hospital that rushes to start work on an unconscious person who has just arrived. The first responsibility is to establish the nature of the injuries before diagnosing the problem and trying to cure it. This is precisely what the team of engineers did.

Modern technology provided members of the commission with a dazzling array of electronic sensors and computers capable of monitoring the health of the tower with unparalleled speed and accuracy. Engineers hooked up sensors throughout

The seventeenth Pisa Commission sent scientists to examine the tower and determine the best way to prevent its collapse.

the tower capable of measuring wind pressure, air temperature, solar radiation, seismic actions, tower tilt, horizontal point movement, moisture levels, dimensional variation in vertical and horizontal sections, width of the cracks in walls and the foundation, masonry temperatures, and the many layers of soil.

Electricians threaded 180 electrical sensors in a variety of critical points within the walls to measure the slightest flicker of movement. In other parts of the tower as well, sensors monitored any changes within the tower night and day. With the assistance of computers that sampled the sensors sometimes once a day and sometimes as often as every second, any change would be documented and used by the engineering team to find a desperately needed cure.

These technical procedures and high-tech tools have revealed the condition of the tower more precisely than anyone thought possible. Measuring sometimes to within a tolerance of $\frac{1}{10,000}$ of an inch, instruments precisely measure and record different types of movement, such as seismometers measuring earth movements, pendulums measuring changes in the lean, inclinometers measuring ground slope, and extensimeters measuring material elasticity. Even the use of a scale model of the tower in a wind tunnel revealed additional information about the vulnerability of the tower in a windstorm. This data has great value to engineers such as Giorgio Macchi, a professor at the University of Pavia, who says of this information, "Nothing must escape. It was that disaster [the Pavia tower collapse] that pushed Pisa toward immediate intervention on the monument [the Tower of Pisa] that, if its inclination increased by another degree, would have collapsed."[14]

One of the earliest successful uses of collected data was the commisson's ability to pinpoint the tower's zone of maximum stress. Engineers built a computer model of the tower by using detailed measurements from the sensors. They were able to calculate structural stress and to highlight its location in blue on the computer model. The engineers learned that although the walls seemed to be solid, many areas had cavities that reduced the strength of the wall.

An understanding of the quality of the masonry, its resistance, and the possible presence of cavities and defects were essential to engineers in determining the risks of structural collapse. The tower's outer surfaces are clad in St. Julian and Carrara marble, but the original builders filled the interior of the

MODERN TECHNOLOGIES

When the Pisa Commission met in 1990, it selected scientists to assist in the restoration of the tower who were knowledgeable in the most recent engineering-measuring and detection equipment. Members of the commission used many types of tools to assess the condition of the tower, including the following technology:

- Sonic tomography: This furnishes a map of the velocity with which sound travels through the walls; the resistance is related to the velocity.

- Thermography: This reveals internal cavities by measuring the differences in temperature between different surfaces.

- Endoscopic televisions: By inserting tiny television cameras into the walls, engineers could peer into the concrete between the two exterior walls to inspect the masonry filling and cavities.

- Flat jacks: These measure the level of pressure in the marble wall facing. This measurement is obtained by making a cut in a horizontal joint between the stone blocks and by inserting a jack; the jack has a sensor in it that then measures the amount of pressure bearing down on it.

- Dynamic identification: By measuring very small vibrations, scientists can identify the minute changes that occur within the tower and its colonnades.

- Radar: Radar reveals cavities and openings via the reflection of electromagnetic waves.

wall with concrete and large, irregular rocks. The use of the large rocks prevented the concrete from completely filling all gaps in the wall. The use of radar on the tower's walls revealed that seismic activity in Pisa over long periods of time had vibrated the walls. These vibrations pulverized some of the rock, causing it to fall into the many gaps the concrete mix had failed to fill. This gradual weakening of the walls placed greater stress on the marble outer surface, causing it to crack and buckle.

Perhaps the most urgently needed measurement determined the extent of the lean. The results indicated that the tower was leaning 5.5 degrees off vertical dead center, meaning that the belfry at the very top extended out over the base by an astonishing 17 feet. A tilt of this magnitude placed too much stress on the old stone walls, especially those at the bottom of the tower, according to soil engineer John Burland: "When we ran our computer model, we found that the tower fell over at [a lean of] 5.44 degrees. But the real tower leans at about 5.5 degrees. That just shows you how close it is to falling over."[15] These careful measurements also revealed that the rate of lean at that time was 1/16 of an inch per year.

Just how close was the tower to falling? Although the scientists could not precisely predict when it would fall, the computer model clearly indicated that it could happen at any moment. The engineers believed that they had to move quickly. They focused on two different objectives. First, they saw the more immediate need to stabilize the tower. This meant simply stopping the rate at which the tower continued to lean. If they could accomplish this, they would be buying time to solve the second long-term problem of reversing the lean and bringing the tower back to a safe position. After considerable discussion, which at times escalated to heated disagreement, the commission proposed three temporary solutions to arrest the continuing lean while working on permanent solutions to reverse it.

THREE TEMPORARY SOLUTIONS

In 1992 engineers determined that the location of greatest stress was on the south side of the second floor. They made this determination by observing a high concentration of cracks in this area, where many of the stone and marble blocks were actually separating. The one-foot-thick marble blocks covering the visible side of the wall were placed here as decoration but also provide much of the tower's support. These observations, along with results from computer models, pinpointed this area as the one most in need of support.

The first of the temporary solutions for this problem was also the fastest and cheapest to implement. Engineers quickly wrapped the walls of the second floor with twelve steel cables that acted like rubber bands to secure these damaged blocks and to prevent them from further fracturing. The twelve

The north side of the Tower of Pisa was loaded with six hundred tons of lead ingots in July 1993.

bands succeeded in squeezing the cracked marble tightly enough to prevent the cracks from widening. Because these cables are an eyesore, they are scheduled for removal once the tower is stabilized.

A second temporary solution was implemented in July 1993. At the recommendation of engineer Burland, the commission agreed to load six hundred tons of lead ingots, acting as counterweights, on the rising north side. The principle was to apply more weight on the high side to slow the rate of lean. The lead ingots were stacked on the north base a few at a time over a four-month period to allow for gradual settling. After the addition of the ingots, the measurements were monitored to see if the desired effect was taking place. By the time all of the six hundred tons had been stacked, the measurements showed that the lean had completely stopped for the first time since careful monitoring had begun. In spite of the success, engineers knew that tinkering on such a large scale might restart the lean or worse—dramatically accelerate it.

The third of the temporary solutions was intended to brace the second floor in the event of a sudden and potentially destructive shift. In May 1998 engineers wrapped a harness of two steel cables around the south side of the second story of the tower and anchored them to counterweights off to the north

In May 1998, a harness of two steel cables was wrapped around the south side of the Tower of Pisa's second story to support it in case of sudden movement.

side. Each cable was 338 feet long and was coated with a heavy plastic sheath. This second story is the same location of the twelve cables already in place. Unlike the twelve cables already wrapped around the second floor to hold the stone together, however, this new harness was designed to prevent the entire floor from exploding outward and collapsing the tower.

At the north side this harness is anchored to a hydraulic winch that controls the harness's tension. Computerized sensors monitor the tension on the cables every four minutes. If the sensors suddenly detect a significant lurch, the computer sends a signal to the winch, which automatically applies or releases the required pressure on the harness. Burland clarifies the purpose for the harness: "The harness is not intended to stop a catastrophic failure, it's not for that at all. It's simply to hold the Tower gently if the movements of the Tower are unexpected."[16]

All three of these temporary mechanical riggings had their detractors. By far, the most frequently heard criticism was that they were ugly and that as long as they were in place, tourists would stay away from Pisa. Instead, however, tourists have continued to flock to Pisa to see the tower as well as to see the rescue attempts that have attracted worldwide attention from the media. The second-most frequently heard complaint was that the cable harness might actually crush the south side of the tower, destroying the delicate marble pillars that surround each of the eight stories. The commission recognized this possibility but felt justified because of the desperate angle of the tower's lean and the distinct possibility that greater damage might occur by doing nothing at all. It was now time for a permanent fix.

TWO PERMANENT SOLUTIONS

The members of the Pisa Commission knew that success would only be achieved after a permanent solution to the continuing lean was found. Initially they had hoped to implement a quick solution by using jacks to raise the collapsing foundation, but they abandoned the idea because computer models indicated that the marble facing that covered the walls would explode outward. Other ideas were explored, but few appeared to be workable. As always, they first tried the option that appeared most promising.

OPPONENTS OF RESTORATION

As surprising as it may seem, many Pisans do not support the attempts by the Pisa Commission to stabilize the Leaning Tower. Those who take this view fall into two different groups: those who fear the tower may collapse in the process and those who believe the attempts may drive tourists away.

Those who fear that the attempts to stabilize the tower may ultimately lead to its collapse are supported by at least one University of Pisa professor of medieval architecture, Piero Pierotti. Pierotti has openly stated his view that not enough is yet known about the tower to begin trying to stabilize it with mechanical contraptions such as the steel cable harness and the 835 tons of lead ingots stacked along the north side. Pierotti and others cite Black Saturday, the night of September 8, 1995, when the tower lurched in that one night more than it normally leans in an entire year. If this could happen one time, they protested, it could happen again and possibly with worse consequences.

Then there is the present appearance of the tower. Tourism is the leading industry in Pisa. Prior to the closure of the tower in 1990, seven hundred thousand visitors hiked the 293 stairs to the belfry for the spectacular views of the city and to experience the world-famous seventeen-foot lean. Many Pisans make their living on the tourist trade in the hotel business, restaurants, or selling the millions of little statues of the Leaning Tower and other souvenirs that tourists take home with them. Many of these vendors and businesspeople fear that tourists will stay away because of all of the engineering work.

Most hated by the citizens of Pisa are the black lead ingots stacked on the north side and the steel harness, both considered eyesores detracting from the beauty of the tower. Jokingly called "the suspenders" by locals, the two steel cables of the harness are wrapped around the tower and are anchored to the ground north of the tower.

Many Pisans believe that after eight hundred years of leaning, the tower will survive another eight hundred without incident and that the government should practice a strict hands-off policy.

UNWANTED ATTENTION

The restoration work on the Tower of Pisa has attracted a great deal of media attention around the world. Not everyone, however, has been concerned with the well-being of the tower. In 1993 the Mafia, a large family of well-organized criminals, planned to blow up Pisa's tower. Fortunately, Italian police officials learned that Mafia leaders planned to explode a 270-pound bomb at the base of the tower and were able to confiscate the bomb and prosecute those responsible. The Mafia had been involved in a series of bomb attacks against some of Italy's most-famous historical monuments. The bombings were being used as a threat against Italy's government to deter their police force from continuing to interfere in the Mafia's illegal activities.

In addition to problems with the Mafia, the thousands of tourists who visit the famed tower each summer attract hundreds of pickpockets. In May 1999 Pisan police spotted several known pickpockets and issued warnings to tourists to protect their valuables while snapping pictures of the tower. Despite these warnings, hundreds of foreign visitors are robbed of their vacation cash each summer. Although most visitors enjoy their stay in Pisa, this trend is alarming to the Pisan police, who are concerned with Pisa's reputation as a favorite tourist destination.

Daredevils, who view the tower as a parachuting opportunity, also cause problems. Parachutists pose a safety problem to themselves as well as to visitors on the ground, who might be struck by them as they descend. Although the tower is closed to the public, parachutists have boldly eluded detection by guards. Stunned tourists recently watched as parachutists jumped before guards could catch them and then escaped in a speeding car before police could be summoned.

ANCHORING THE TOWER

In 1994 the commission made the decision to attempt to permanently anchor the high north side of the tower deep into the ground with ten vertical cables placed under tension. To attach the ten steel cables to the tower, the first job was to pour a new circular foundation 165 feet below the north side of the existing foundation poured by Pisano eight hundred years ago. Once the new foundation had hardened, ten steel cables on the north side of the tower would be attached to the new foundation and anchored into a compacted layer of sand and bedrock deep below the surface. Geologists' tests had confirmed that this bedrock was significantly denser than the softer and wetter mud and clay found at shallower levels.

The chairman of the commission, Michele Jamiolkowski, believed this solution to be feasible with help from the existing twelve steel cables and lead ingots. The plan was first to dig a trench around the tower to give excavators access to the soil and bedrock below the existing foundation. The plan then called for excavations into the bedrock under the north side to scoop out

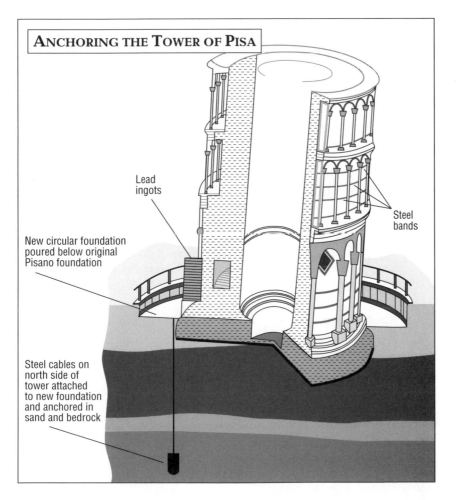

ANCHORING THE TOWER OF PISA

Lead ingots

Steel bands

New circular foundation poured below original Pisano foundation

Steel cables on north side of tower attached to new foundation and anchored in sand and bedrock

Workers at the Tower of Pisa prepare for an excavation under the tower.

room for the concrete anchor. Once all debris was removed, machines would pump concrete into the 13-foot-wide and 6.5-foot-deep semicircular hollow. Engineers would then attach ten steel cables, connecting the high north side of the tower to the new concrete anchor that was bonded to the bedrock 165 feet below the base. The tension on each cable would be adjustable, and each cable could withstand one hundred tons of pressure.

If all elements of this plan proceeded as scheduled, engineers would finally apply pressure to the ten cables to first stabilize the tower and then to begin to reverse the lean. Engineers

BLACK SATURDAY

All engineers working on the project to stabilize the tower knew that fiddling with this leaning 14,500-ton giant posed certain risks. These risks became evident on the night of September 8, 1995, when excavations around the base suddenly caused the tower to lurch nearly one-tenth of an inch. The sensors in the tower that monitor the most minute movement suddenly sent signals to the computers as if a major earthquake had struck the site.

One-tenth of an inch had been the average movement for an entire year, and to have a movement that great happen in one night was terrifying. No one knew if the lurch would be repeated several nights in a row, leading to the collapse of the tower. To stabilize the tower, 235 additional tons of lead ingots were added to the 600 tons that engineers had begun gradually amassing on the rim of its base in 1992 as a counterweight. In fact, engineers were so desperate to prevent additional tilt that they actually parked the crane used to lift the ingots on the north side of the tower alongside of the ingots.

Things had begun to go wrong that night when the ground, frozen for the installment of the anchoring device, went haywire. Apparently, the use of liquid nitrogen, which was needed to freeze the moist earth to prevent it from compressing any further, backfired when some areas froze and others did not, causing a sudden lurch in the tower's tilt.

One expert who was highly critical of the plan was Piero Pierotti, a professor of medieval architecture at the University of Pisa and a man considered by many to be the world's leading historian of the tower. Pierotti argued that the project was badly conceived from the start by engineers who failed to take the time necessary to understand the risks involved in the proposal to anchor the north side of the tower.

Fortunately, this one lurch did not repeat itself. However, ideas of anchoring the north side of the tower and the use of liquid nitrogen were both abandoned.

USING THE TOWER AS A LABORATORY

An interesting side effect of the restoration work to the tower has been its use by modern scientists as a laboratory for experimenting with new engineering technologies. Before twentieth-century advances in science and engineering, no experiments were performed on the tower to attempt to arrest or correct its lean. Some people even thought that the tower's dramatic lean was an act of God because they had few scientific tools with which to understand its cause.

During the twentieth century, and especially during the 1990s, scientists using the site as a laboratory have learned a great deal about soil, foundations, and walls—information that can be applied to other threatened structures as well as to structures planned for construction.

The Tower of Pisa has provided an excellent laboratory setting because the scientists working on the site have had many years to study the structure in a relatively safe environment. Geotechnical engineers have examined in painstaking detail the soil under the tower's foundation to understand the cause of the lean. Today's soil engineers speak about soil characteristics in terms of

estimated that they would be able to pull the 193-foot-tall tower back one inch per year from its lean and to stabilize its lean sixteen feet off the vertical axis.

In midsummer of 1995, the excavation work began on the project. Removal of the soil and bedrock went smoothly, and the engineers believed they had hollowed out a good foundation for the concrete anchor. Workers then injected liquid nitrogen, at a temperature of 321 degrees below zero, into the moist soil above the targeted area for the anchor to freeze and harden any groundwater that might collapse the excavated hollow intended for the concrete.

As engineers began to pump the concrete into the new foundation on September 7, 1995, things began to go very wrong. As engineers started pumping the concrete through several hoses down to the anchor site, the computerized sensors began to go berserk, detecting more movement than thought possible. The sensors recorded a lean that night equal compaction, expansion, bearing capacity, and shear—all terms that would have been foreign to twelfth-century builders. After studying the soil and foundation problems in Pisa, one of the questions posed by modern engineers was whether current theories of building on moist subsoil could have prevented the famous lean. The answer to this question is a surprising "not necessarily."

The reason modern engineers cannot necessarily prevent similar leaning problems in future construction is because of what they call "limits of failure." This term means that every element of a building has structural limits that, when exceeded, will cause failure. In the case of the tower, these limits of failure apply to the ability of the soil to support the tower's weight, the soundness of the tower's basic design, the quality of the concrete foundation, and the amount of concrete in the foundation. All of these limits can be measured today and can be met. There is, however, one factor that cannot be controlled: the continued unpredictable heaving of the soil in the Piazza dei Miracoli as a result of rainfall and the underground stream movements. Because of this factor, it is conceivable, although unlikely, that the tower may one day begin to lean in an entirely different direction.

to the lean for the previous entire year. Burland explains the incident this way: "As we began to freeze, the tower began to move and we stopped the work. To control the movement we rather urgently added another 235 tons of ingots and at one point the crane itself."[17] Jamiolkowski suspended work until the commission could meet to reevaluate the plan. Following their meeting, the commission canceled the plan to anchor the north side of the tower. A different, less risky approach would need to be found.

Jamiolkowski and other members of the commission had run out of plausible solutions until they learned of a technique successfully used over a four-year period to stabilize the Metropolitan Cathedral in Mexico City, which had developed a tilt of over six feet as a result of settling. The solution there had been to slowly extract soil from under the high side of the cathedral, causing it to settle over time. At this point, the Pisa Commission was willing to try anything.

A drilling rig extracts small amounts of soil from the high side of the Tower of Pisa in an attempt to reduce the tower's lean.

SOIL EXTRACTION

In February 1999 soil engineer Burland ran computer models and field tests until he and other engineers on the committee were convinced that extracting soil from the high side would lower the fragile tower gently back toward normalcy without a disaster. The principle was to gingerly remove small amounts of soil from beneath the high side of the tower, creating an underground maze of holes almost as if burrowing rodents lived there. As the soil was removed, so went the theory, the weight of the tower could gradually collapse the holes, allowing it to gently settle.

To excavate soil beneath the tower, workers drilled with an eight-inch auger blade inside a specially designed casing through which the soil was extracted at the surface. To avoid introducing potentially destructive vibrations, the actual drilling rig was situated about seventy feet away from the tower and bored the holes at a thirty-degree angle. Burland explains the process this way:

> If we look at this [the bore holes], the soil will then close in the cavity and we'll see the Tower rotating back towards the north side as we under-excavate. A 10% reduction in inclination will reduce the stresses by 10% in the masonry, and that's a very reasonable amount.[18]

Beginning in March 1999 with twelve bore holes over a width of only about 18 feet, Burland and his crew removed underlying soil at the cautious rate of about 2 cubic feet per day. By mid-June, the team had bored more holes, and the tower had leaned back toward the north by about one inch at the top; by August the lean had corrected by 1.5 inches.

By June 2000 the success of the soil-removal solution had corrected the lean by a remarkable 5 inches following the extraction of 250 cubic feet of soil. On June 17, to celebrate the success of the project, officials opened the tower for one day for the first time in ten years, allowing one hundred schoolchildren

THE WRANGLE OVER THE ANGLE

As though there were not already enough dissention within the engineering committee working on the tower about whether to attempt the stabilization, more dissent broke out amongst those who support the stabilization of the tower over just how much they should attempt to correct the famous lean.

As work to remove earth under the north side of the tower began, the question arose as to how much of the lean should be left, if any at all. When discussions about correcting the lean began in 1990, when the tower was first closed, citizens of Pisa as well as thousands around the world were horrified by the thought that the tower might actually be straightened to a perfectly vertical axis. Most people familiar with the seventeen-foot lean could not imagine the tower without it and began to lobby to stabilize the tower but not to remove the lean.

Citizens of Pisa who admired the beauty of the tower also recognized realistically that, without the dramatic lean, it was highly unlikely that tourists would continue to flock to Pisa to photograph the tower and to spend their money on souvenirs and restaurants. The question then became how much lean could be left and still make the tower safe enough to reopen to visitors.

As preparatory work began on the plan to lower the north side by slowly extracting earth from beneath it, many wondered how much of the seventeen-foot lean would be removed if the plan worked. Michele Jamiolkowski, chairperson of the Pisa Committee, believes that if sixteen inches of the lean can be corrected, the tower will be safe for visitors for another three hundred years. Part of this estimate was based on the hope that the sixteen inches would be corrected in time to celebrate the new millennium.

For the time being, it appears that the correction of between sixteen and twenty inches proposed by Jamiolkowski will remain the target unless engineers decide that more is necessary to make the tower safe for visitors.

to climb the 293 steps to the top. In September 2000 workers removed three tons of the lead ingots in anticipation of the eventual progressive removal of all of the ingots.

Engineers on the project estimate that to achieve the goal of reducing the inclination 10 percent, another 450 cubic feet of soil will need to be extracted. They hope to complete the project by the summer of 2001, when the reduction of the lean should reach 20 inches. Burland believes that "the soil extraction fix should last about 300 years."[19] Burland warns, however, that if soil needs to be removed every five years, the plan will be unreasonably intrusive. If, however, the soil only needs to be removed every three hundred years, this preservation plan will be excellent.

Will these engineers continue to remove soil until the tower is straight? Absolutely not. The intent is not to straighten the most famous leaning building in the world, it is to make the tower safe for the return of visitors. Besides, the tower can never be perfectly straight because its tilting in different directions over the years caused designers to compensate by building one side taller than the other, giving it a slightly curved profile.

EPILOGUE

The engineers on the Pisa Commission have established a mechanical solution that could potentially correct the lean of the tower back to a perfectly vertical position. Should that be their objective? After all, that was precisely what Pisano intended when he designed the tower and began construction in 1173. Why then, has the commission decided to correct the tower a mere 20 inches and leave the lean at about 15.5 feet?

The answer partly rests with engineering considerations and partly with the economic considerations of Pisa. Computer models have shown that considerable risks abound when a tower such as Pisa's is straightened out. As the upper floors are pulled back, increased stress on the lower floors might cause walls to crack and upper floors to topple over. After carefully reviewing the computer models, the commission determined that a sixteen to twenty-inch correction would safely stabilize the tower without incurring further risk of catastrophic proportion.

The commission was also responsive to the financial impact that the tower has on the economy of Pisa. The commission knew very well that a straightened tower would not continue to attract seven hundred thousand tourists a year who contribute millions of dollars to the local economy in hotels, restaurants, and gift shops. Everyone recognizes that the tower's attraction is its lean, not so much the aesthetic qualities of its Romanesque style of architecture. Without the lean, the city of Pisa would simply be one of many small, picturesque university towns dotting the northern Italian landscape.

Considering all of the risks involved in the Pisa project, perhaps it is fair to conclude that the Pisa Commission has performed remarkably well. This project to stabilize the tower and to learn many engineering lessons has proved to be a unique opportunity for the members of the commission. The ten years have not been without controversy and sleepless nights. Lead engineer Jamiolkowski made this comment as the tower began to correct its tilt following the soil extraction, "Fear has accompanied us always. Each time we touch the Tower it is enough to make one worry. I hope that it finishes in a hurry, and maybe then I will leave. I will return to Pisa like a tourist to see it again with new eyes."[20]

The Pisa Commission has decided not to straighten the tower because of engineering considerations and because of the impact that the tower's lean has on the city's economy.

If all continues to go well, Pisa will celebrate the summer of 2001 with festivities befitting the tower's return to good health. This project has not only brought satisfaction to the citizens of Pisa, but it has also brought a wealth of information to the international engineering community that will be useful on future similar projects.

Notes

Chapter 2: Towers

1. Aeschylus, *Agamemnon*. Trans. Richmond Lattimore. Chicago: University of Chicago Press, 1959, pp. 35–36.
2. Percival Price, *Bells and Man*. Oxford, England: Oxford University Press, 1983, p. 112.
3. Quoted in Joseph and Frances Gies, *Life in a Medieval City*. New York: HarperPerennial, 1969, p. 144.
4. Price, *Bells and Man*, p. 134.
5. Price, *Bells and Man*, p. 139.

Chapter 3: Initial Construction Phase

6. Quoted in Tania Marchesini, ed., *The Leaning Tower*, doctoral thesis, 1999. http://humanities.cisiau.unipi.it/~pierotti/Torre/Speiser.html.
7. Quoted in Marchesini, *The Leaning Tower*.
8. Gary Feuerstein, "The Unofficial English Language Tower of Pisa Website," 1998. www.endex.com/gf/buildings/ltpisa/ltpisa.html.
9. Feuerstein, "The Unofficial English Language Leaning Tower of Pisa Website."
10. Quoted in *NOVA*, "Fall of the Leaning Tower," PBS broadcast transcript, October 5, 1999.

Chapter 4: Final Construction Phase

11. Quoted in Robert Kunzig, "Antigravity in Pisa," *Discover*, August 2000, pp. 72–79.
12. *NOVA*, "Fall of the Leaning Tower."

Chapter 5: Modern Restoration

13. *NOVA*, "Fall of the Leaning Tower."
14. Quoted in Feuerstein, "The Unofficial English Language Leaning Tower of Pisa Website."
15. Eli Kintisch, "Balancing Act," *Popular Science*, July 2000, p. 57.
16. Quoted in *NOVA*, "Fall of the Leaning Tower."
17. Quoted in Domenico Pacitti,"Professors with Learning Difficulties," *Guardian* (London), August 19, 1997.

18. Quoted in *NOVA*, "Fall of the Leaning Tower."

19. Quoted in *NOVA*, "Fall of the Leaning Tower."

Epilogue

20. Quoted in Feuerstein, "The Unofficial English Language Leaning Tower of Pisa Website."

FOR FURTHER READING

Books

Xavier Barral I Altet, *The Romanesque Towns, Cathedrals, and Monasteries*. Cologne, Germany: Taschen, 1998. This is a superb work that provides a comprehensive history of Romanesque architecture as well as numerous full-color, detailed photographs that illustrate the major architectural elements.

Joseph and Frances Gies, *Daily Life in Medieval Times*. New York: Black Dog & Leventhal, 1999. This is an update and expansion of the Gies's book *Life in a Medieval City*. It depicts a broad swath of everyday life and includes wonderful full-color photos and reproductions of medieval art.

Hans Erich Kubach, *Romanesque Architecture*. Milan, Italy: Electa, 1988. An excellent book on Romanesque architecture, covering all of the major and some of the minor elements. This book is richly illustrated and includes sketches of many of the structural elements that lend greater understanding to the reader.

Corrado Ricci, *Romanesque Architecture in Italy*. London: William Heinemann, 1925. This work has one of the better discussions of the function and structure of towers in the Romanesque style. It also contains excellent architectural drawings and black-and-white photos.

Periodicals

Paulo Heiniger, "The Leaning Tower of Pisa," *Scientific American*, December 1995. This article is without question the best magazine article dedicated to the engineer work involved in the restoration effort. It contains excellent drawings and graphs describing the tower and engineering problems encountered in the restoration process.

Websites

La Torre di Pisa, Official Website: http://torre.duomo.Pisa.It. This is billed as the official website for the Leaning Tower of Pisa. Its primary strength is its extensive collection of sixty-four hundred photographs of the tower that provide the viewer with the ability to look at the details of the architecture.

Gary Feuerstein, "The Unofficial English Language Leaning Tower of Pisa Website," 1998. www.endex.com/gf/buildings/ltpisa/ltpisa.html. This wonderful website, billed as the unofficial website for the Leaning Tower of Pisa, is loaded with translated articles from newspapers and magazines related to the Tower of Pisa. Its primary focus is on the restoration attempts of the past ten years.

WORKS CONSULTED

Books

Charles II. Acland, *Medieval Structure: The Gothic Vault.* Toronto, Canada: University of Toronto Press, 1972. This book provides wonderful insights into vaulting and how builders planned the structural elements that were needed to support the vaults. It also discusses problems with estimating heights and lengths of vaults and includes excellent cross sections of buildings that illustrate how they are supported.

Aeschylus, *Agamemnon.* Trans. Richmond Lattimore. Chicago: University of Chicago Press, 1959. This play tells the tragic story of King Agamemnon's war against the Trojans and the misfortunes that followed.

Joseph and Frances Gies, *Life in a Medieval City.* New York: Harper Perennial, 1969. This is an excellent anthology of information about the day-to-day life in a typical medieval city, encompassing family life, business, education, religion, and government. It provides a wonderful cross section of a person's life during this time.

Percival Price, *Bells and Man.* Oxford, England: Oxford University Press, 1983. This is a fascinating book on the history, sizes, and uses of bells in both Western and Eastern cultures. It contains information on the evolution of the bell tower as well as discussions about some of the most famous bells and their histories.

Charles M. Radding and William W. Clark, *Medieval Architecture, Medieval Learning: Builders and Masters in the Age of Romanesque and Gothic.* New Haven, CT: Yale University Press, 1991. This is primarily an academic work discussing the work of architects and the builders of the great buildings of the Middle Ages. It provides fascinating insight into the thought and planning required to complete the masterpieces of this historical period.

Periodicals

Eli Kintisch, "Balancing Act," *Popular Science,* July 2000.

Robert Kunzig, "Antigravity in Pisa," *Discover,* August 2000.

Domenico Pacitti, "Professors with Learning Difficulties," *Guardian* (London), August 19, 1997.

Internet Sources

Tania Marchesini, ed., *The Leaning Tower*, doctoral thesis, 1999. www.cisiau.unipi.it/~pierotti/Torre/index-en.html. This website is a doctoral thesis containing many references to documents on the Tower of Pisa contained in the University of Pisa's library. All articles are translated and are organized into the following four categories: historical background, documents, press cuttings, and discussion and comments.

Other

NOVA, "Fall of the Leaning Tower," PBS broadcast transcript, October 5, 1999.

INDEX

PICTURE CREDITS

Cover photo:(Clockwise from left) Gary Feuerstein; PhotoDisc;
    Erich Lessing/Art Resource, NY
© Alinari/Art Resource, NY, 10
© Paul Almasy/Corbis, 20, 23
AP Photo/Riccardo Dalle Luche, 96
© Archivo Iconografico, S.A./Corbis, 69
© Bettmann/Corbis, 16, 43
E. C. Jones & Associates, 12, 26 (left and upper right), 33, 81
© Ric Ergenbright/Corbis, 29
© Owen Franken/Corbis, 86
© Marc Garanger/Corbis, 26 (bottom)
© Historical Picture Archive/Corbis, 70
Hulton Getty/Archive Photos, 17, 37, 40 (right), 62, 68
© Erich Lessing/Art Resource, 19, 42, 61, 74
© Michael Lewis/Corbis, 82
© Lawrence Migdale/Photo Researchers, Inc., 24, 25
© North Wind Picture Archives, 60, 65
© Reuters/Carlo Fabbri/Archive Photos, 92
© Reuters/Vincenzo Pinto/Archive Photos, 100
© Reuters/STR/Archive Photos, 87
© Scala/Art Resource, NY, 36, 49, 51, 55, 57, 58, 73, 79
Martha E. Schierholz, 15, 53, 91
© Ted Spiegel/Corbis, 18
© Stock Montage, 66
© Telegraph Colour Library/FPG International, 40 (right)
© Sandro Vannini/Corbis, 44
© VCG 1999/FPG International, 48
© Adam Woolfitt/Corbis, 30

ABOUT THE AUTHOR

James Barter received his undergraduate degree in history and classics at the University of California (Berkeley) followed by graduate studies in ancient history and archaeology at the University of Pennsylvania. He has taught history as well as Latin and Greek.

A Fulbright scholar at the American Academy in Rome, Mr. Barter worked on archaeological sites in and around the city as well as on sites in the Naples area. He also has worked and traveled extensively in Greece.

James Barter currently lives in Rancho Santa Fe, California, with his fifteen-year-old daughter Kalista who enjoys soccer, the piano, and mathematics. She hopes to attend either Yale or UCLA although her father hopes she will consider Berkeley. His older daughter, Tiffany, lives in Kansas City where she plays violin with the Kansas City Symphony.